How to Be a Minister

and a

Human Being

Harold C. Warlick, Jr.

Judson Press ® Valley Forge

HOW TO BE A MINISTER AND A HUMAN BEING

Copyright © 1982
Judson Press, Valley Forge, PA 19481

The Scripture quotations in this publication are from the Revised Standard Version of the Bible copyrighted 1946, 1952 © 1971, 1973 by the Division of Christian Education of the National Council of the Churches of Christ in the U.S.A., and used by permission.

Library of Congress Cataloging in Publication Data

Warlick, Harold C.
  How to be a minister and a human being.

  Includes bibliographical references.
  1. Clergy—Office.   2. Clergy—Mental health.
I. Title.
BV660.2.W37   1982   253'.2   82-8926
ISBN 0-8170-0961-2   AACR2

The name JUDSON PRESS is registered as a trademark in the U.S. Patent Office.
Printed in the U.S.A. ⊕

For Diane,

my wife and friend,

and Scott,

my son and teacher

Acknowledgments

The idea of exploring in depth the personal and professional dilemmas and triumphs of ministers came originally from my work on a course at Harvard Divinity School entitled "Introduction to Ministry." As I struggled along, with various of my colleagues, to find textbooks that would introduce our new students to the realities, both personal and professional, inherent in the ministry, it became clear that much diverse material needed to be brought into a more structured framework and much original research needed to be done. Harold Twiss, general manager of Judson Press, suggested the development of this material into book form. His encouragement and advice led to the birth of the book.

I join many other ministers in owing a debt of gratitude to Charles Merrill, whose financial generosity and personal commitment to sabbatical leaves for clergy, made possible the Merrill Fellowship program at the Harvard University Divinity School. As director of the Merrill Fellowship program I have come to know well the personal lives of many of America's outstanding ministers. In addition, I feel that I have been privileged to be an "insider" in their congregations.

Several people helped shape portions of this book by their helpful suggestions. The Reverend Bobbie McKay, Ph.D., a registered psychologist in Winnetka, Illinois, provided insight into recurrent problems in the family life of the minister. James Luther Adams, Mallinckrodt Professor of Divinity, Emeritus, at Harvard Divinity School, provided helpful material as did Michael Coogan, associate professor in Old Testament, Harvard Divinity School. My friend and colleague, David Shi, professor of history, Davidson College, was most instructive in telephone conversations and letters on the subject of voluntary simplicity.

I thank the students in my courses at Harvard Divinity School who challenged me to prepare for publication much of the material in this book and the ministers in the Doctor of Ministry program, Union Theological Seminary, Richmond, Virginia, whose enthusiasm in a course I taught there and subsequent responses to my research enabled me to move forward better informed and encouraged.

I am grateful to Ruiko Connor who spent patient hours deciphering my handwriting and typing successive manuscript drafts.

Finally, and most important of all, much love and gratitude to Diane, my wife, and Scott, my son, who fit my writing so lovingly into their own schedules.

Harold C. Warlick, Jr.

Contents

Introduction

The purpose of this book is to examine the problems and potentialities associated with developing meaningful relationships and a sense of purposeful activity in the profession of the ministry. Few vocations demand such a powerful expression of the sense of personal identity as does the ministry. (Religious faith, of course, is a personal identity issue for all religious persons, even those in professions like law and medicine. But law and medicine *as professions* do not demand the vocational expression of the personal identity of the practitioner in the way that ministry demands it from the minister.) I am convinced that many clergy pay a heavy price in terms of happiness and fulfillment in their professional lives, with their self-images, and with their family lives for not admitting their loneliness in the ministry, facing it, and grappling with it honestly. Loneliness becomes pathological when it is not recognized, worked through creatively, and managed effectively.

I hope that in the following pages we can step back together and examine some of the basic guidelines, attitudes, myths, problems, and principles that direct the activities of the professionals called "ministers" and condition the kinds of responses ministers make in specific circumstances.

Certain dangers exist, as always, in attempting to analyze a profession as a whole. Some might argue that my attempt to understand the profession is doomed to failure because ministers and their vocational expressions are as varied and specific as the individuals who labor in the profession. Others might argue that my concern for parish ministers is too traditional and narrow. Still others might reason that assumptions and attitudes about ministers of churches should be left tacit because exposure to direct scrutiny could lead to dissension.

In answer to the first two arguments I will readily admit that ministry is no less individualized than any other profession. No one solution can be found to the complex personal and professional problems that beset the ministry in its rapidly increasing specialization. On the other hand, we belong to a "profession" which has earned and lost certain images, attitudes, and perceptions through its functioning in American society. To deny that would be to deny a part of who we are. I believe it is profoundly important to move beyond the specificity of personal analysis and speak of the ministry as a whole. People recognize in other professions, which are just as diverse as the ministry, that beyond Officer Jones there are the police; that beyond Dr. Smith there is an American Medical Association; that beyond Ms. Norman, there are lawyers; and that beyond Representative Stanford there are politicians. The societal attitudes toward police, doctors, lawyers, and politicians profoundly affect the individuals who practice those professions. In the same way societal attitudes affect the individuals who practice professional ministry, and it is important to identify some of the problems, attitudes, and potentialities that impact this profession.

My response to the third argument is to agree that the direct scrutiny of ministerial assumptions could lead to dissension. My personal belief, however, is that unspoken assumptions about the ministry often degrade the quality of our lives, narrow our vision to self-serving ends, and lead to a sense of malaise that becomes chronic because the courage to delve to the heart of the difficulties is lacking. I can only hope that my methods of exploration have been responsible ones.

Finally, allow me to posit the obvious. I have written this book through the colored lenses of my own experiences, perceptions, triumphs, and failures as a minister and, as such, claim only to be a fellow practitioner who owns and affirms both the mess and the joy of ministry. The audacity of one who is not a clinically trained psychologist writing this work perhaps warrants some explanation. I have sought to touch base with the universal struggles and triumphs of ministry by utilizing as much first person experience, both my own and others, as possible. My perspectives and conclusions have been supported by and in most instances shaped by data collected from Protestant ministers in twenty-two states.

A detailed questionnaire was completed by fifty ministers who provided in-depth responses concerning their personal and professional triumphs and failures. In examining the issues of self-image, professional identity, and family life, I especially wanted to avoid studies that have been conducted by psychologists and denominational executives. Such studies tend to analyze "problem" clergy and treat certain pathological trends as absolute for the profession. I, however, sought to target "successful" clergy for the survey and utilized former Merrill Fellows from Harvard University Divinity School as well as personal acquaintances to compile the mailing list. (Less than 10 percent of the ministers invited to participate in the research possess a degree from Harvard University Divinity School.) Only ministers currently active as members of the senior staff in a local church were utilized. A copy of the questionnaire, along with more specific information about the research, is to be found as an Appendix at the end of the book.

Certainly the sensitive personal information shared by these ministers made this book a reality. Their willingness to "lay bare" their personal and professional lives has enabled me to draw some startling conclusions about the joy and pain in ministry, conclusions which contradict prevalent findings and myths encouraged by other authors and researchers. I am glad that these colleagues trusted my discretion in handling sensitive personal information. I have quoted them as often as possible in the book in order to enable them to tell their own stories.

It is hard to overestimate the importance of sharing with one another our struggles, pains, and healings. I hope that I will be able to lay bare some of the particularities of our profession in a way that will enable you, the reader, to see more clearly your own pain and joy. In a significant and honest way I hope to evoke for you a freeing experience, one that will give you greater insight into the depth and complexity of the profession to which we have been called. This book is meant to offer you courage and healing, enabling you to see more clearly the meaning and challenge of our lives as ministers, professionals, and family members. Thus I write as a minister to ministers.

Carl Rogers, one of the most insightful and innovative psychologists in our era and a prime advocate if not the founder of nondirective counseling, said recently that only one kind of counselee is relatively helpless—the person who blames other people for his or her problems. Rogers contends that if we can own the mess we are in, there is hope for us and help available. But as long as we blame others, we remain a victim for the rest of our lives. Too often psychoanalysis has reinforced a sense of hopelessness. My efforts to confront openly the problem of ministerial loneliness are predicated by my desire to see our profession "own the mess" of ministry and affirm our power to choose who we will be and what we will be. Consequently, I do not seek to find an illness in ministry, give it a name and prescribe a treatment.

Loneliness in the ministry will perhaps always be with us. However, in the midst of that loneliness we can emphasize the importance of our own self-acceptance and develop some guidelines, however tentative and flexible, for a more productive management of its symptoms. At the very best, this effort will help us toward a healthier combination of positive regard for ourselves as ministers and an awareness of our limits. At the very least, this effort should enable us to communicate more authentically who we are and to lessen the stress of our ministry by operating assertively with our parishioners and our families out of heightened self-awareness.

Part One

The Minister's Self-Image

1

The Job: Divine Burden or Mission Impossible?

The signs of the times are everywhere. "Job dissatisfaction: Growing every day" reads the heading of a major newspaper article by Fern Schumer, syndicated columnist of the *Chicago Tribune*. The Schumer article quotes Department of Labor studies which found that perhaps as many as 11 percent fewer people found their work interesting in 1977 than did in 1969. "There's isn't enough room at the top for all of us. So many get stuck with the routine chores, the unexciting work with no upward mobility," says Robert Schrank, program officer with the Ford Foundation. "'In the '80s, it's going to get worse,' says Robert Quinn, associate research scientist at the University of Michigan's Survey Research Center."[1]

What's true of society in general is an even more acute situation in the profession called "ministry." Denominational offices are working feverishly to complete studies on clergy morale, which appears to be at an all-time low. In fact, one such study of 149 ministers in Pennsylvania found that 84 percent of them had experienced low morale which affected their work as ministers.[2]

If ministers are to understand and manage their ministries in times like these, they must first of all manage what consultants for business executives call "the self-system."[3] Ministers who wish to manage effectively their self-systems must develop an understanding of that system and its processes. The goal of this chapter is to examine the contrasting expectations and the lack of understanding about the work of the ministry. This lack of understanding creates incredible loneliness in the lives of ministers.

A Definition of Loneliness

For our purposes it seems appropriate to define loneliness as "the absence of purposeful activity and meaningful relationships." Consequently, loneliness differs from aloneness, which is defined as "not being in the company of other humans." Therefore, marriage can be a lonely experience when it has lost its meaning. Some of the loneliest people in the world are the most active, futilely searching for something that will give them purpose.

It is difficult to define the ministry. Clergy have the kind of job that is ripe for lack of meaningful relationships and purposeful activity. They structure their own time. They do not have a single supervisor closely observing their performance. They usually work alone in the performance of their task; and there is a list of unwritten expectations they are supposed to know but to which they have not formally agreed in writing. They are expected to be professionals.

A professional is defined as "one who engages in a calling requiring specialized knowledge and often long and intensive academic preparation." Sociologist Adam Yarmolinsky defines a professional as one who has "special knowledge, special skills, special resources, and special responsibility."[4]

The minister is both a professional and a generalist. Ministers teach but must solicit their own classes. They heal, but must do so without pills or a knife. They are sometimes lawyers, sometimes social workers, sometimes editors, sometimes entertainers, salespersons, decorative pieces for public functions, and are supposed to be scholars. They visit the sick, marry people, bury the dead, admonish the unethical, and try to stay sane when criticized. They plan programs and appoint committees when they can get volunteers.[5] And they never have the choice *not* to preach.

In the ministry there exists little clear separation between work, family, recreation, and personal privacy. The job is not universally understood, and ministers have very few things they can measure at the end of the day to be sure of their accomplishments. Added to these problems are the problems of dealing with the contrast in job expectations between the professional and the lay person.

In spite of the incredible demands and pressures in the profession of ministry, C. S. Calian reports that people are disappointed in pastors who show "emotional immaturity and actions that demonstrate immaturity. . . ."[6] Likewise the *Readiness for Ministry*[7] studies produced the following result: The most significant characteristic or criterion that people across denominational lines are seeking in their young clergy is "service without regard for personal acclaim." This "describes an individual who is able to accept personal limitations and, believing the gospel, is able to serve without concern for public recognition."

Is it any wonder that the job of ministry appears less like a divine call and more like an impossible mission? Reviewing the expectations, demands, and lack of role clarity experienced by clergy, Dr. Margaretta Bowers, a psychotherapist who treats ministers with problems, remarked, "Columbus sailing westward seeking to find China knew more precisely where he was going than do these [clergy]."[8]

I'm not *that* pessimistic about the profession and would refrain from making categorical statements on the basis of a few case studies of clergy in psychotherapy. But I will admit that the profession of ministry carries with it some incredible burdens. In fact, when we combine the inherent dangers in the profession with the increased loneliness in the society of which we all are a part, the complexity of the minister's situation is apparent.

Loneliness is not a philosophical problem spoken about mainly by writers and poets. Suzanne Gordon, author of *Lonely in America*, called loneliness "the new American tradition."[9] The strong relationships that affirm who we are are getting harder for people to find. We have reached the point where the average American moves *fifteen* times in his or her lifetime and over 55 percent of the adult population lives more than five hundred miles from their places of birth and childhood roots.

The medical profession acknowledges something ministers have seen in their parishioners' lives for a long time—loneliness produces serious medical consequences. James Lynch, a specialist in psychosomatic medicine at the University of Maryland Medical School, has shown how lack of human contact can affect a person's cardiac system. His book, *The Broken Heart*, evidences that people with secure, stable lives and strong personal ties to others are far less likely to fall prey to disease than those who experience less companionship.[10]

Diminished Awareness of Purposeful Activity in Ministry

I suppose my first hint of the fact that many individuals possess distorted stereotypes of ministers came in my very first month in the ministry. At that particular time I was pastoring a church in the little city of Seneca, South Carolina. The day had been a long one in terms of my ministry. An early morning ride to the hospital with a parishioner whose daughter had been in a horrible automobile accident had been followed by two involved and draining counseling sessions with young couples who were perched on the edge of divorce. By noon I had already worked eight hours and had not even begun the normal routine of sermon preparation, visitation, and preparation for committee meetings. And, tired as I was, I had to eat a quick lunch because I had arranged for one of the church members, a banker, to accompany me on an early afternoon visit to his mother in a nearby hospital.

The banker was an incredibly busy man and could not always visit the hospital during the hours normally set aside for family visitation. Consequently, I had arranged for him to accompany me on the thirty mile trip to the hospital and use one of my chaplain's badges to "assist" me in making a pastoral call.

As we emerged from the chaplain's room in the hospital lobby, I handed him a badge that said "Reverend Harold Warlick" and half-jokingly said, "Now, try to act somewhat like a minister because it's not regular visiting hours." With a big smile he looked at me and replied, "Don't worry. I'm lazy and I love fried chicken!"

"I'm lazy and I love fried chicken!" We laughed over his punchline for several minutes. But as we drove back from the hospital that day, I kept wondering how many times that joke had been told in washrooms, boardrooms, and restaurants around the South, if not around the country. I must confess that for as long as I have ministered in churches and universities, I have never since that day ordered fried chicken in a public place when the menu afforded me another choice!

Since that day I have encountered, even among my colleagues in theological education, a number of jokes with the same meaning— "if business gets bad, you can always take up preaching." I share with Edgar M. Grider amazement at how our profession with its twelve-hour or more work days can be the target of the common assumption that the ministry is for those who can do nothing else or that the ministry is something anyone can do. Grider further observes

> that such humor places ministers on the second team—or third, or fourth! The first team is out there playing the game, while the minister is seen on the sidelines, retired from the field as it were: cheerleader at best, idle bystander at worst."[11]

Such humor indicates the incredible problems associated with the profession. Perhaps no other profession finds itself so trapped by contrasting expectations and distorted stereotypes. Small wonder that many ministers succumb to the strong temptation to let "the role" prescribe and define their personalities and actions.

". . . We are brought into this world by a group . . . and we are carried out of the world by a group," says Bowers in *Systems of Organization*. Somewhere between the obstetricians (or midwives) and the pallbearers (or crematorium assistants), we have to live with other groups for a long time. We are shaped and formed through our encounters with the groups in our lives. Consequently, the problems inherent in the public perception of ministers directly influence the self-image under which ministers operate.

David Bowers is an organization specialist in secular business. He works with companies to see that they effectively organize and manage human resources. He has noted that three groups have the greatest influence on peoples' lives: the family, the work groups, and the group of closest friends. Bowers notes that "we spend one-third of our adult lives interacting in the family setting, one-fourth in the work group, and only perhaps one-tenth in recreation or interaction with our closest friends."[12] Consequently, if executives do not find purpose and meaningful relationships with their work group, they may not find an answer for loneliness.

If we rightly consider the minister's work group to be his or her parishioners, then I would contend that a minister spends more than the secular one-quarter of adult life interacting with the work group. Probably one-half to three-fifths of the adult life of the minister is spent with the work group. Herein lies a great problem. A minister's work group, as the *Readiness for Ministry* studies show, simply does not envision the minister's work the way he or she does. The documented disparity between lay perception of ministry goals and clergy perception of goals is a tremendous contributor to lone-liness. Frankly, many ministers are not finding their activity to be as purposeful as it was perhaps in earlier generations—the erosion of consensus concerning the minister's role and the church's purposes over the past thirty to forty years has been a debilitating burden to carry.

Consider, first of all, the media. The omission of the minister from popular children's literature and television is evident. "Who are the people in your neighborhood . . . the people that you meet each day?"[13] goes the familiar children's song. Sesame Street and its literature catalogue meet all the visible community professions—except the ministry. Nowhere is the minister, priest, or rabbi to be found. Likewise Richard Scary's popular children's books illustrate everything in the world of Busytown from showmaker to newspaper editor to lumberjack. The minister is not included. As Russell Richey in "The Missing Minister" has noted, the world as given to young children by television and literature has excluded the minister.[14] All of the challenge of ministerial service, the accomplishments and peril, the importance of what we do—all that is being excluded from American life as it is portrayed in children's literature.

Peter Raible is a Unitarian minister in Seattle. In his article, "Images of Protestant Clergy in American Novels," he has traced the ministry in literature from _Moby Dick_'s Father Mapple of New Bedford through the Industrial Revolution—when the male minister was often viewed in the feminine role of nurturer, safely removed from the masculine marketplace where the wheels of business churned and the changing money clinked—to the modern day. He notes rather convincingly that in one hundred years of literature the image of the parson as the preeminent leader gave way to the image of the ministry as a refuge for those who were disinterested or incompetent.

Raible points out that few contemporary novels portray a Prot-estant minister with any professional understanding or depth. Con-sider the omissions. No novel centers on a Protestant minister as a social reformer. Truman Nelson uses as a basis for _The Sin of The Prophet_ (1952) the life of Theodore Parker but Nelson's book is more a biography than fiction. Secondly, no novel attempts a serious portrayal of a female Protestant clerical character, in spite of fa-vorable portrayals of Catholic nuns. Aimee Semple McPherson appears only in an autobiography. Biographies and autobiographies are not generally shapers of thought as fiction writings are.

Raible notes, thirdly, that American fiction largely ignores the black minister. James Baldwin alone has written of the black minister, and he writes in a way that lampoons evangelical preachers who have no formal training rather than supports an image of a more heroic type.[15]

Yet more novels have been written about Protestant clerics in the past decade than ever before. These either lampoon the minister or deal with ministerial professional efforts in a narrow way. John Updike in *A Month of Sundays* includes a sermon that is a defense of adultery and eventually has the minister protagonist sent off to a clerical rest and rehabilitation center. A recently published novel, *The Miracle*, has as its central character what it calls, "the best known evangelist in America." He is an expert at amorality and has a more corrupt cleric son. The story conforms to the outward facts of Billy Graham's rise to success as an evangelist.

Consider another example in the fifty years of popular fiction's lambasting of clerics as simply flashy showpersons, moral shams, and frauds—the novel and the film, *Oh God!* Even Frederick Buechner's *The Final Beast* (1965) and Charles Mercer's *The Minister* (1969) present the Protestant minister as a fairly dull person attempting to work in rather unimaginative ways. At best, fiction shows ministers winning out against oppressive or domineering congregants. The church is depicted as an ossified institution bucking and resisting every move toward peace, tolerance, and caring, an enclave for the bigoted who delight in restricting or unmasking the clergy.

While in fiction today no cleric is taken seriously as a public opinion maker, intellectual, or cultural leader, ministers have been written about. Eberhard and Phyllis Kronhausen's work, *Pornography and The Law* notes:

> Many "obscene" books . . . have among their central figures persons connected with the clergy and religion. . . . These "holy" individuals are then depicted as engaging in highly tabooed sexual activities.[16]

The ministers' work group, the laity in the country, are bombarded with these images in the media. While the laity most probably discount or neutralize many of the negative images, I think it is a true statement that laity habitually do not appreciate or understand much of the purposeful activity in this profession. Certainly our media-oriented culture does not hold up before children and laity the office of ministry in the way that the oral culture of another generation did. Whatever reinforcement is given for respecting the ministerial role is given by in-house denominational and ecclesiastical bodies. Cults and the Unification Church in particular capitalize on the breakdown of respect for the ministry in their communications with the young.

In my survey of fifty ministers, the question was asked, "Do you believe that your congregation understands and appreciates what you do as a minister?" Forty-eight percent (twenty-four respondents) flatly stated that their congregations do not understand what they do as ministers. An additional five respondents stated that their congregations appreciate but do not appear to understand what they do. For example, a young minister (thirty-year-old male) reports that the people appreciate the "visible" aspects of ministry, such as preaching and teaching, but have no recognition of the enormous preparation time needed for these activities.

A thirty-nine-year-old male minister with fourteen years' experience in the ministry responded to my question:

> Each member has a different idea of the primary role of the minister. For some, I'm to be a great preacher (a Fosdick), to others a great counselor . . . , to still others a caller, an administrator, a church bureaucrat, a friend, a social activist, etc., etc. There is a core of people who understand the complex demands and the many hats, but most people do not see the daily round for what it is.

Another thirty-nine-year-old male minister with nine years' experience in the ministry reported, "The older members, with more traditional expectations about the role of a minister, often have the least understanding and appreciation of what we actually do."

Finally, a thirty-year-old female minister with three years' experience in the ministry responded, "They have a different set of values than I and have differing expectations of what I should be doing."

The Search for Professional Identity

When one's work is not understood by the persons for whom it is done, a deep and abiding professional loneliness occurs. The professional is often tempted to think that his or her work has little value and may seek to perform in ways understood by the "consumer." Sometimes the latter results in clergy creating nonexistent needs to which their generally perceived resources are the answer. A kind of professional insecurity develops.

Ralph McInerny in a novel called *Gate of Heaven* gives a clear example of the type of loneliness produced by professional insecurity. The story is set within a retirement home for priests. One of the characters is the aged and retired Father Stokes who spends most of his days going to the local airport and having himself paged over the public address system. Listen to one of Stokes' scenarios:

> A commercial jet approached from the east, most likely from Cleveland. Stokes leaned on the railing and watched it come down, tons and tons of machinery gliding to earth as gracefully as a feathered bird.
>
> The jet had taxied to the terminal and now stood on the ramp below him. Passengers were disembarking. The luggage train drew up beside the plane. He turned and stepped to the pay phone behind him. He rang the number of an airline counter on the main floor below.
>
> "Would you have Father Stokes paged, please? It's very important."
>
> "Would you repeat that?"
>
> He repeated it, spelled his name.
>
> "Is he on our flight?"
>
> "I'm sure he's in the terminal."
>
> "I'll page him."
>
> "Thank you."
>
> He hung up the phone and started for the stairway. He came into the main waiting room with the sound of his name reverberating. There was a nice note of urgency in the pager's voice. Father Stokes assumed an expression of concern and hurried through the crowd. One or two faces connected his clerical figure with the announcement that had just been made. There were lines at the counter but he caught the eye of one of the clerks and raised his brows quizzically.
>
> "Are you Father Stokes?"
>
> "Yes, I am."
>
> The man beckoned him forward. People stood aside. "There was a call for you, Father. Funny thing; they seem to have hung up." He presented the phone to Stokes. The old priest held it to his ear.
>
> "Curious," he said. "No one's on the line. Did it seem important?"
>
> The man shrugged. "I'm sorry, Father." Stokes turned. Again the people parted to let him through. He went to the waiting room and sat down. Everyone would now know that there was a priest in the terminal. Perhaps someone would have need of him. He

could easily be found, sitting there. He opened his topcoat, to make sure that his Roman collar was visible.

He should have left the phone upstairs off the hook. A simulated conversation would have made an impact. Some poor devil on the verge of suicide, desperate for discussion. Of course he would telephone Father Stokes. Just an outside chance that he might be caught at the airport. A busy man, always on assignment by his society, please God, let him be between planes. Only his voice on the phone could restrain the hand of despair. *Sed tantum dic verbo* . . . A tiny plane dropped in for a landing and Father Stokes smiled at it, a proprietary smile, the smile of a man on the ready. Fear not. The plane landed safely. Stokes relaxed. He was not needed. Yet.[17]

While the account of the life of Father Stokes and what Ronald Rolheiser calls Stokes' "fantasy-loneliness" are but good fiction, I must confess that I think of Father Stokes sometimes when I encounter the reliance of our profession on clinical pastoral education. Are we not often, like Stokes, using another institution's switchboard to self-page our ministerial identity?

Rollin J. Fairbanks contends that ". . . The clinical and professional insecurity of the clergy in America today . . . [has been] an influential factor which has led to an unconscious over-identification with other more popular and respected healing professions." Fairbanks continues, "The struggle to retrieve or to re-create a unique professional identity or self-image continues."[18]

This helps to account, in my opinion, for the disproportionate influence wielded by clinical pastoral education on denominational ordination requirements. Each year I research the requirements among the denominations which provide Harvard Divinity School with the majority of its students: American Baptist, United Presbyterian, Presbyterian Church in the U.S., Lutheran Church in America, American Lutheran Church, Episcopal Church, United Church of Christ, Methodist Church, and the Unitarian-Universalist Association. As incredible as it may seem, seven of these denominations either require or strongly recommend a basic unit of clinical pastoral education, but only *one* (Unitarian-Universalist) requires any knowledge of or courses taken in world religions!

I recognize the tremendous importance of counseling skills in ministry. But is not a small but important motivation for the over-emphasis on clinical pastoral education the desire to identify with a respected secular healing profession? Shouldn't we desire to be able to articulate Christianity intelligently on the world scene? If we are secure and stable as a profession, is it not incredible in the times in which we live that we do not provide leadership in personal and societal decision-making in a rapidly shrinking world?

In writing these words, I have been fearful of offending you, the reader. Please understand that I value clinical pastoral education as well as education for ministers in public policy, politics, and business. However, I also recognize the struggle for pastoral ministry to "stand on its own," to affirm itself as a profession apart from other professions. This must not be done in proud isolation but with a necessary and enriched understanding by its constituents of congregants that the ministry has a centered existence distinct from other professions.

In both seen and unseen ways, ministers must struggle daily for a greater degree of self-determination. They must try to free themselves from the prison of an inadequate self-image. I envision at least two ways to do this: 1) accepting more theological responsibility for oneself and one's ambitions, which I will discuss later in the book; and 2) informing one's work group of the work one actually does. This would define pastoral ministry for what it is instead of leaning on other professions for legitimacy and identity. This latter point is crucial for viewing one's work as "purposeful activity."

Informing the Work Group

It appears to me that a certain weapon against loneliness in ministry is the minister's active attempt to inform the work group about the specific work of the ministry. The minister must have a positive impact on the shaping of lay perceptions—those of both adults and children. Such involvement cannot be imperialistic, and it consists of more than just making denominational literature on the ministry available (which even so may not focus on the specific tasks of pastoring a church). The work of ministry must become more valued and more understood.

In my job as director of ministerial studies at Harvard University Divinity School, I have worked with ministers from thirty-eight denominational and religious traditions. For four years I have directed a program for clergy on thirteen-week sabbaticals from their churches and parishes. Even in this program, which brings together some of the most successful ministers in the world, I find the same situation: *Few ministers have actually systematically tried to teach their congregations what ministers do.* Many congregations know something about their minister's function, but what they know, from tradition and media, is probably inaccurate and incomplete. Whatever the means, from preaching a series of sermons about one's work to conducting special study groups, ministers must teach their work group about their work.

An effective procedure for informing laity of one's work is to invite people to one's home or parsonage in small groups for the express purpose of learning more about the pastor's work. Small groups in a living room can discuss informally over coffee the totality of the ministerial functions. I prefer to do this outside of committee meetings and social occasions. My goal is to invite four groups of twelve people each to my residence every year for a two-hour discussion of my work in the ministry. Over a period of four years I have gained two hundred lay persons who better understand my work.

Another effective instrument for educating laity about the nature of the ministerial task is the adult education program of the church. Special classes and seminars in "What Does a Minister Do?" need to be held every few years. Remember, many people are operating around a conception of ministry that is decades old. Others have formed their conceptions in a composite manner, taking a few items from the job descriptions of every minister they have ever known. These seminars or classes need to be held every four to five years because the minister's tasks change as the needs of the church change. A minister often performs a different ministry in his or her fifth year than in the first two years. Churches need to be frequently updated as to the work of their minister.

Efforts to inform the work group (laity) of the actual tasks in ministry usually produce a two-way street for appreciation and assistance. The best example I have seen in this regard came from the experiences of a Baptist minister in the state of Virginia. At the gracious invitation of Pat Miller, dean of Union Theological Seminary, in Richmond, Virginia, I taught a course there one summer in parish development and management. Following the course, one young minister asked if I would continue to consult with him concerning some internal problems within his membership. This particular pastor was experiencing intense personal and professional stress, much of which came from the fact that the membership possessed little awareness of his actual work load.

Our initial efforts took place with the twenty members of his official board (diaconate). For each monthly meeting the minister prepared a time log which he discussed with the board, and he also targeted a particular facet of his ministry for discussion in each meeting. He reported to me some helpful suggestions offered by the laity concerning time management and personal setting of priorities. Especially helpful were homemakers, who, of course, manage their "self-system" in ways far better than many of us care to admit. In addition, he reported that most of the lay leaders came to the realization that their conceptions of ministerial tasks were outdated.

A new sense of understanding and trust developed between the minister and the diaconate, resulting in the development of mutually agreed upon expectations of performance and role. The lay leaders themselves began to assume responsibility for many of the tasks which the minister had been doing. The minister decreased his working hours from an average of sixty-two hours per week to an average of forty-eight. But equally important, he began to feel less isolated in the routine performance of his ministry, knowing that at least twenty individuals in the congregation understood, affirmed, and appreciated his work. The task remaining for that minister and the church leadership is to devise ways to inform the rest of the work group about the nature and value of the tasks being performed in their midst.

While informing the work group is certainly no panacea for professional loneliness in the ministry, it certainly appears to be the best place to begin. The United Church of Christ study of morale among Pennsylvania clergy concluded that the "most important factor in precipating low morale . . . is poor lay-clergy relationships."[19] The same study also focused on the need for clergy and laity to be seen as a unit in a parish. It posited that an "oversight is made in most of the present strategies offered for helping clergy cope with low morale. They deal with clergy in isolation from laity, in counseling sessions, career development seminars, continuing education events, etc. Very little effort is directed at helping clergy and laity together. . . ."[20]

William Glasser in *Reality Therapy* noted that every person has basic physiological and psychological needs. "Psychiatry must be concerned with two basic psychological needs: *the need to love and be loved and the need to feel that we are worthwhile to ourselves and to others.*"[21] It is difficult if not impossible to feel worthwhile to one's work group if it does not understand one's work. Ministers can, like the fictional Father Stokes, continue fruitlessly to page themselves through available opportunities or continue to over-identify with secular professionals in the hope that some of the respect and trust afforded them by laity might rub off on the ministry. Or, ministers can take positive steps to inform individuals whose concepts of pastoral work may be outdated or negative at best. I believe that the latter avenue is better for helping ministers solicit others' affirmation and understanding of the divine burden (not mission impossible) which they bear on their shoulders.

2

Loneliness, Stress, and Clergy Burnout

*"How do I minister to people in crisis when I am in
crisis myself?" (A minister to the author)*

I had always liked Henry. In many ways he served as mentor for
several of us who were studying in the Master of Divinity program
at Harvard Divinity School. Henry was in his mid-forties and had
several "successful" New England pastorates under his belt. In addition, he seemed to be on the right side of most of the compelling
social issues of the day. My friend and fellow seminarian, Joe, used
to spend hours in my dormitory room discussing with me the latest
cause in which Henry was engaged. Joe and I were so impressed
with Henry's commitment to ministry that we contracted to do our
field education work in the church in Massachusetts where Henry
was a member. At that particular time Henry was employed by a
denominational agency in downtown Boston working on the problems of the urban poor. We envisioned lively dialogue and profound
stimulation, working with the church committees on which Henry
served.

And for six months, the vision was lived out. Henry's pastoral
sensitivities resolved many impasses in committee meetings and his
pastoral experiences came through to us in many diverse ways. In
Joe and me Henry had two eager and aspiring adherents, anxious
to adopt him as a model for our own careers in the ministry.

I'll never forget that cool October morning when Joe came to my room in Divinity Hall and knocked on the door. "What's happening?" I asked him. "Just come here and take a look," he implored.

I threw on a bathrobe and ran down the steps to the lawn in front of the dormitory. There, on the lawn, was parked an old pickup truck with its motor still running. In the bed of the truck lay much of Henry's entire library, over five hundred books on the subjects of religion, ministry, and counseling.

Slowly and painfully, Joe turned his face toward me and with a blank look in his eyes said, "Henry quit the ministry. He called me and said he'd had it with the ministry and would never be coming back to it. He wanted you and me to have his books and asked that I come right then to get them because he's on his way out of town."

So, on the dew-covered grass of Divinity Hall, Joe in his pajama top and blue jeans and I in my pajamas and bathrobe divided up a large chunk of Henry's life in the ministry. As we tossed around the Tillich, Barth, Otto, and von Rad, I understood much less about clergy burnout than I do now. All I knew was that Joe, the ministry, and I had all lost a good friend. And that Henry had lost a part of himself.

Hundreds of ministers like Henry fall victim each year to clergy burnout. These clergy expend considerable effort, their intensity reaching a point of exhaustion, often without visible results. The military calls it "battle fatigue." Clergy, and others in similar situations, "feel angry, helpless, trapped, and depleted: they are burned out. This experience is more intense than what is ordinarily referred to as stress." Harry Levinson, writing in *Harvard Business Review*, points to the major defining characteristic of burnout as, "people can't or won't do again what they have been doing."[1] This certainly appears to hold true for the ministry. Edgar Mills and John Koval conducted a major survey of 5,000 Protestant ministers in 1971 entitled *Stress in the Ministry*. They noted that 24 percent of the ministers dealt with stress by changing jobs,[2] often getting out of the ministry entirely and into another profession.

Ministers, of course, are not unique in the professional stress which they encounter. Business executives are also prone to stress through some of the same conditions that ministers face.

Professional Stress

A pioneer researcher on stress, Christina Maslach of the University of California, Berkeley, has documented the stress-produced syndrome of "burnout." Characterized by emotional exhaustion and cynicism, it is frequently experienced by people in "people-work"— for example, poverty lawyers, physicians, prison personnel, psychiatrists—who spend considerable time in close encounters with others.[3] Harry Levinson states in the *Harvard Business Review:* "Managing people is the most difficult administrative task, and it has built-in frustration."[4]

Consequently, ministers can in no way claim they are the only professionals who walk a tightrope among the conflicting interests of human beings. In fact, the Levinson study of business executives lists characteristic situations among managers with which most ministers can readily identify. The situations:

> Promised great success but made attaining it nearly impossible.
> Exposed the managers to risk of attack for doing their jobs, without providing a way for them to fight back.
> Aroused deep emotions—sorrow, fear, despair, compassion, helplessness, pity and rage. To survive, the managers would try to harden outer "shells" to contain their feelings and hide their anguish.
> Exploited the managers but provided them little to show for having been victimized.
> Aroused a painful, inescapable sense of inadequacy and often of guilt.[5]

The advice that Levinson gives for managers is "to talk together, often with a group therapist or someone else who can help them relieve some of the irrational self-demands they frequently make on themselves as groups and as individuals."[6] We will attempt to consider this advice later in this chapter in the subheading, "The Need for a Controlling Purpose."

While we must admit that ministers suffer many of the same symptoms as all professionals who do "people work" and that ministry is by no means the only highly vulnerable occupation, it remains that certain types of stress are unique to the profession of ministry. In the Mills and Koval study, nearly two-thirds of the ministers attributed their stress to problems related solely to the job of ministry.

Previous research has dealt with a number of particular stress-related problems in the ministry.

Blizzard (1958) found that work time demands upon Protestant

ministers were highest for tasks they enjoyed least and felt ill
prepared for. . . . Campbell and Pettigrew (1959) studied ministers
in a stress-producing racial integration situation. They found that
internalized values of justice and equality were reinforced by denominational . . . leaders, but that these were unable to help the
clergyman deal with the conflict and stress generated by his support of racial integration.[7]

Thus ministers felt trapped between denominational expectations
and local realities.

Hadden (1969) recognizes an "identity crisis" in the Protestant
ministry today and attributes it to the growing conflicts between
pastors and laymen over authority, belief, and purpose in the
church. . . . Jud, Mills and Burch (1970) report . . . stress arising
from family situations, a sense of inadequacy, job placement problems, work frustrations and personal illness. . . . Stress in the
ministry is attributed by Biersdorf (1971) to 'the churches' inability
to respond adequately to change.[8]

The aforementioned study by Mills and Koval in 1971 identified
the major form of stress in the ministry as being personal or ideo-
logical conflict with parishioners.[9] I believe that James E. Dittes also
saw the phenomenon of resistance in the parish as the precipitating
factor in clergy stress in his study, The Church in the Way (1967).
Donald P. Smith also confirmed resistance and conflicting expectations in the parish in his 1973 work, Clergy in the Crossfire. Finally,
the major surveys in the Readiness for Ministry volumes (1977)
pointed to conflicting role perceptions between clergy and laity as
a major cause of ministerial problems.

Positive Stress

Stress, of course, is not always unpleasant and unhealthy. On
the contrary, stress can be beneficial. Many of us perform best when
under stress. The diversity of the ministry, for example, seems to be
both a stressful and a positive aspect of the profession. Sam Blizzard
has written that for the professional in a voluntary institution such
as the church, role diversity and a lack of clarity of what is expected
should not be surprising. Donald Smith, building on this finding,
notes that some men and women who are exhilarated by opportunities to use problem-solving skills are actually attracted to such
situations. Smith contends that narrowly defined and rigid job def-
initions might limit the creativity of a minister and actually undercut

the motivation of some of the best men and women in the profession.[10]

My survey of fifty ministers certainly confirms this contention. By a wide margin the respondents indicate that the most attractive feature of the ministry for them is its diversity. Twenty-seven respondents, or 54 percent of the total, answered the question pertaining to the most attractive feature of ministry in this way. The response was the same from both male and female clergy.

Among the many positive responses in appreciation of ministerial diversity were these:

The most attractive feature is its diversity.

Few other professions allow one person to do weekly public speaking, counseling, programming, social action, education and administration . . . I seem to be a person that needs to be a generalist . . . I don't like narrow specialization. (thirty-nine-year-old male minister with fourteen years' experience.)

The diversity and profundity tap all my energies and skills and involve and push my intellect. (forty-one-year-old female minister with four years' experience.)

Ministry encourages growth, personally and socially. Included is the opportunity to explore and experiment with new living forms. (sixty-four-year-old male minister with thirty-six years' experience.)

Doing many different tasks; some alone and some in groups. (twenty-eight-year-old female minister in her first year of ministry.)

The problem seems not to lie in the *presence* of stress in the ministry but in the fact that little is understood about the sources of and solutions to stress in the ministry. While not all ministers find the stress in their ministry to be overwhelming, there are limits to the degree of role conflict that a person can take. Ministers need a more self-conscious understanding of their work so that they can exercise more control over the ambiguities relating to their particular place of service.

If one chooses to accept as inevitable certain stresses in ministry or chooses to maintain them on the basis of a professional calling, that is an acceptable manner of performance. One knows the personal and social costs involved in such a profession. But if a minister is trapped in stresses and ambiguities that he or she did not anticipate and cannot manage, that's quite another matter. Coping becomes impossible.

Stuart G. Leyden, pastor of the First Presbyterian Church, Wankesha, Wisconsin, has written an article entitled, "Coping with Stress." He posits that "in order to cope with stress successfully we need to feel that we have some control over our lives."[11] Certainly a sense of control is a major factor in managing ministry. The aforementioned tactic of keeping the work group informed can enable a minister to be in charge of the perceptions about ministry that are operating in his or her church.

Leyden's conclusion is that one will cope with stress more ably if one is intentional in one's choices. Fortunately, the profession of ministry presents some privileges that enable ministers to shorten the distance between the professional and his or her work group.

The ministry is the last profession that has retained the privilege of *initiative and access.*[12] Over the centuries ministers have worked for and won the privilege of initiating relationships with others. Even medicine and law no longer have access to clients' homes and crucial moments in their lives. Perhaps the greatest discovery I made in leaving the local church ministry for the university was that I had lost identification with a profession which entitled me to call casually in people's homes and have access to their stressful times and significant moments.

Ministers can utilize this privilege not only to inform the work group but actually to control better their use of time. The fact that the ministry is a "self-initiating" profession demands that a minister exercise self-understanding and self-discipline with respect to time. The ministry is one of the few professions left in society where the leader can structure his or her time to a significant degree.

Half of all clergy work more than ten hours per day. As a professional group, ministers are *overly-consumed with their own work and their own sense of importance.* Such overconcern usually can be traced to the aforementioned loss of a sense of purposeful activity. Keeping busy often makes a minister feel less vulnerable to criticism in a job that few laity understand. It also enables a minister to feel needed for certain routine, mechanistic procedures, partially alleviating the great fear of lack of purposeful activity.

R. Alec Mackenzie has written that "executives who consistently devote more than forty-five to fifty hours a week to their jobs are in serious danger of impairing their efficiency. Several studies have established that productivity declines rapidly after eight hours of work." MacKenzie cites Robert Pearse of Boston University who calls this the myth that "the harder one works, the more he or she gets done . . . the buckets-of-sweat syndrome." Instead of being a catalyst for productivity, "intense activity frequently acts as a protective reaction against insecurity. . . ." The French cavalry have a motto: "When in doubt—gallop!"[13]

Much of the stressful "galloping" that ministers do comes from inadequate theological and personal understandings. Ministers experience problems in terms of identification. "We identify high. Anyone who identifies with the God of all Creation and purports to be called to do God's work will have a lofty sense of responsibility and perfectionism. It's not quite the same as manufacturing widgets or repairing light fixtures,"[14] as Lloyd Rediger, Wisconsin Council of Churches, says.

The Totally Available Minister

A persistent theme that comes through previous studies on clergy stress, in both its positive and negative manifestations, is the "always available" nature of ministerial life. This factor makes ministerial stress different from stress found in other professions in which persons are not available at all times.

Ministers should recognize that anxiety, which leads to loneliness, increases as the level of exposure and amount of personal availability increase. Local pastors constantly bear the brunt of other peoples' anxiety and change as do few *if any* other professionals. Local pastors are *totally available to other people.* It has apparently always been this way. The apostle Paul wrote of this in his second letter to the church at Corinth: "And apart from other things, there is the daily pressure upon me of my anxiety for all the churches" (2 Corinthians 11:28). And of the village pastor Oliver Goldsmith said, "He watched and wept and prayed *and felt for all.*"[15]

No other profession calls for such rapid transitions between joy and sorrow. A wedding may follow upon a funeral with only several hours' interval. Henry Sloane Coffin wrote that "Christians must be everlastingly at the work for the commonweal which God appoints them; and they must bear the weights of fellow-mortals who jar on them, the pressures of the winds of current thought which sweep upon them, and the subtle changes in climate to which they are exposed every twenty-four hours and every year of their lives."[16]

Ministers, unlike other professionals, are called upon constantly to stand in the face of death—the final and ultimate threat to personal being—and enable themselves and others to both accept and triumph over the deep sense of loss and grief. Many ministers face this situation several times a week, year after year.

Anxiety intensifies as the personal investment and identification increase. Since the anticipation of the minister's own death is always in the background of every grief situation, the very process of being a minister puts that man or woman "in touch with needs, . . . and discrepancies in his [or her] own private life." As Cecil R. Paul has noted, "This continued self-consciousness brings to the minister a whole new inner-directed dimension of stress."[17]

Ministers have *initial* contacts with more people seeking assistance with stress than all other helping professions combined. The minister is the first line of defense for a host of personal and domestic problems.

Perhaps more than any other profession, ministers are totally available to the inequities of *poverty and wealth.* Ministers are constantly aware of the incredible gap between poor and wealthy parishioners. Other professionals are less aware of the financial diversity among their clients than are ministers. False guilt can easily tear apart a minister who is totally available to the extremes between wealth and poverty.

Let me illustrate the kind of stress caused by this total availability with an example from my own ministry.

One of the switchboard operators at the county hospital in the community where I pastored belongs to our denomination. She wasn't a member of the church I pastored, but she was aware that I am usually willing to care for people who are in desperate need of financial and other services.

During one of my rare evenings at home with my family, the telephone rang, and I recognized the voice of my friend at the hospital switchboard. Her voice reflected the exasperation she obviously felt. She began her story, "There are two men here at the hospital who want to see a minister. I do not know what they want, but they say they need to see someone within fifteen to twenty minutes."

I tried to calm my friend and assured her that I would arrive at the hospital in due time and try to assist the gentlemen.

My feelings of bitterness at having to leave home came to the forefront in a matter of minutes. I had been settled in my favorite chair, looking forward to an evening with my wife and infant son, and now I was giving up that pleasure for two people I had never met.

Mumbling and grumbling, I arrived at the hospital. The switchboard operator pointed me in the direction of two elderly gentlemen standing by a water fountain. If ever I had seen persons in destitute circumstances, these two men were prime examples. Their clothes reflected the style of another generation. Both were unshaven and unkempt. One walked with a slight limp, and the other was so undernourished I was surprised he could walk as well as he could.

The one with a limp approached me. "Pastor, our mother has just died, and we don't know what to do. Her body is upstairs, and we don't have any money to even bury her. Can you help us?" Thus began an experience which caused me to rethink my perspective on the subject of guilt.

As we made arrangements for the county to help cover the expenses of the funeral, I learned more of the background of this pair of needy persons. The two men were disabled, one through epilepsy and the other through tuberculosis. Their disability and welfare checks could not meet the rapidly accelerating cost of living.

Through the kindness of a Christian funeral director, we arranged for the minimal services to be obtained. A florist in our church donated a spray for the casket. The cemetery owners donated a lot in their grounds.

On the day of the burial the mortician called to ask me if I could help him carry the casket from the hearse to the grave since there would be no one else but the two disabled men at the service. As we lugged that heavy, plain container through the South Carolina red clay, I felt uneasy inside. These people didn't deserve their misfortune any more than I deserved my good health. It just didn't seem fair. The poverty, loneliness, and despair inherent in the situation overwhelmed me. I began to feel what many Americans experience when they view the poverty of the world—guilt over having been born privileged.

It took me two years to work through the stress caused by this one incident. In fact, I became so obsessed by my need to come to terms with the stress of guilt that for those two years I spent two evenings a week in the Clemson University library reading every article and book I could find on the general subject of "guilt." One Saturday a month for an entire year I traveled to Decatur, Georgia, to use the library at the Candler School of Theology at Emory

University. My research reached manuscript proportions and was published as a book so that it could be of assistance to other clergy.

Obviously a minister cannot place such energy and time into attempting to resolve every impasse that comes unannounced into her or his life. Yet I was amazed at the sheer number of ministers who wrote me long letters in response to reading the book. Many commented how their total availability to such discrepancies between wealth and poverty had negatively affected their ability to minister effectively to certain parishioners and had even led them into negative self-images.

Another critical stress that emerges from the minister's total availability to others is the stress produced in counselor-counselee relationships with members of the opposite sex. Unfortunately the research on the subject of sexual intimacy between ministers and parishioners is very limited. Certainly the minister, male or female, is a sexual human being and must make himself or herself available to parishioners at times when the minister may also be a burdened person. Perhaps the minister's own needs for pleasure are blocked, or the minister's state of relationship with her or his own spouse is not particularly strong; no matter, the totally available minister is still on call to the personal problems of the opposite sex.

Ann Bartram teaches pastoral counseling in the Toronto School of Theology. She has conducted research on the topic of sexual intimacy between the pastor and parishioner. Bartram reports that in her own private practice she was carrying at one point a client load that included eight women, all of whom had had some kind of sexual relationship with the minister they were seeing for counseling! Bartram further states that there is very little data when the female is the minister and the male the parishioner.[18]

My own research among ministers confirmed much of Bartram's findings but also provided evidence of sexual problems when the counselee was a male minister and the counselor a female parishioner. To protect the respondent, I will identify him only as a middle-aged male minister with over fifteen years' experience in the ministry:

> Out of loneliness and despair over several frustrations in my life, I opened up and talked and shared with one of the members of my church—a counselor and a woman. The relationship just simply got out of hand and into the bed. It's over now. Looking back I see the good but I think I understand all of the complexities

involved in getting involved. . . . It's not just a . . . man in mid-life crisis reaching out for a little comfort and reassurance—it's a minister. . . . I've had all that lovely "free love" lavished on me for years. At least in this relationship there was some equality. I was equal for the first time. . . . I feel loneliness now more than ever and I don't know who to talk to. I lost my friend with the affair. I also learned a lesson over again—don't get too close. Keep that pulpit distance . . .

Consider the incredible stress placed on a professional who must always know his or her own emotional vulnerability! Consider also what it must be like to be the spouse of a minister, knowing that your spouse must be totally available to relationships in which sexual feelings are likely to become strong.

A thirty-two-year-old male minister articulated it well in his response to my question concerning the ways in which the profession of ministry hampers family life in ways that other professions wouldn't.

The concentration of activity on evenings and weekends puts me out of the house when other people are having their family times. This makes my wife lonely and sometimes angry; and sometimes it makes me feel intensely guilty. The preponderance of women I deal with as a pastor is a real cause for conflict, though not always overt: my wife gets to feeling that other women are drawing on my limited reserves of affection and compassion, and she isn't getting her just share.

No less than eight respondents used the word "mistress" to refer to the way their wives view their relationship to their church. Two female ministers, aged thirty-nine and forty-one, referred to the same problem in their relationships with their husbands.

One of the major findings in my survey of ministers is that female ministers find the impact of the ministry on their spouses to be as difficult as the impact of the ministry is on the spouses of male ministers. A fifty-four-year-old female minister with twenty years' experience in ministry responded in these words:

Perhaps you need to be concerned not only with the loneliness of the minister but with the loneliness of the spouse, too. In my first marriage, I feel I was not sufficiently understanding of my husband's needs. I was wrapped up in the excitement and interest of a new career in a fascinating field. I was involved with lots of people who were satisfying a lot of my ego needs. . . . My husband started going around with other women who had more time for him. in retrospect I can hardly blame him.

A thirty-one-year-old female minister with four years' experience in the ministry writes in the questionnaire that being a minister hindered her relationship with her husband. She states that people kept telling him how "talented his wife was. . . . That's hard on anybody." Finally, a thirty-four-year-old female minister indicated that being single only enhances the problem. While she finds that many men will come to her for counseling, she also finds that men are more hesitant to ask a woman minister for a date. It's a difficult dilemma.

Perhaps stress impacts all institutions negatively and positively, and each professional experiences stress differently. Yet I can think of no more stress-prone profession, no line of work where psychological stress is more pervasive or more acute than in this profession of total availability called the ministry. Acceptance of this fact is a precondition for any hope of successfully managing one's life in the profession.

Preventative Medicine

No less a person than Jesus of Nazareth recognized the stress factors involved in being totally available to conflicting expectations. Luke's fourth chapter reports that following Jesus' announcement that the Spirit of the Lord had anointed him to preach the Gospel to the poor, preach deliverance to the captives, and set at liberty those who are oppressed, the hearers began to say, "Is not this Joseph's son?" (Luke 4:22). Jesus anticipated their line of attack and said, "You will surely say unto me this proverb, 'Physician, heal yourself.'" The meaning, of course, is clear. Why couldn't Jesus do miracles in his home town as he did elsewhere? The Christ responded with his famous words that no prophet is accepted in his own home town.

Persons tend to call upon ministers to "heal themselves" when they face personal limitations; the attempt to do this is a temptation to which many pastors succumb. Edgar W. Mills and John P. Koval, writing on the subject of stress in the ministry, reported that among the five thousand respondents, "About two-thirds of the stress periods were met with independent efforts to master the problem by [themselves]!"[19]

I firmly believe that the place to begin is to accept the stress that accompanies the totally available nature of the ministry and build into the job description resources adequate to the need. A minister should not be required to practice self-healing for all potential and real problems.

I believe that each congregation should place in its annual budget a sum of money for "staff personal enrichment." As part of accepting the call to the church, each minister should agree to have a psychological consultant, of his or her own choosing, paid for by the church from the aforementioned fund. No other staff member or church member, except perhaps the person who signs the checks, needs to know the identity of the consultant. But I believe ministers should be required to make use of those monies annually. Many corporations now require their executives to have regular consultations with psychologists and other professionals because of the stress of working in "people work." As I have attempted to show, the ministry contains all the stress inherent in corporate work as well as the requirement of total availability, which far exceeds any stress in the corporate world.

In my years of dealing with churches, both as a minister and as a placement officer for students graduating from divinity school, I have encountered over one hundred churches looking for a minister. Many of those churches have required the ministerial candidate to have an initial physical examination and then, once they have hired someone, required the minister to have a physical examination annually. In addition, an increasingly large number of these churches required the candidate to allow them to employ professional companies to conduct credit checks. But I have yet to encounter a church or parish that makes available to the minister church funds for the employment of a psychological consultant to help the minister perform effectively in a stress producing profession. Perhaps I have experienced an unrepresentative sample and most churches are actively engaged in such endeavors. But I doubt it.

3

Personal Ambition and the Ministry

"The power to reject or disregard power is itself an expression of power." (James Luther Adams)[1]

Ministers as a group are similar to people in other professions. Ministers' weaknesses and strengths are just as weak and strong as others'. If anything distinguishes ministers from other professionals, it lies in what they expect of themselves and what others expect of them. Ministers are called to stand strong in the face of life's outrageous assaults, to point to hope in the midst of death, and to speak for justice when others are afraid to speak. They are expected to do this for an entire lifetime; yet the work group (see chapter 1) seeks individuals who give "service without regard for personal acclaim."

Thus the minister appears to be caught in a trap. On one hand, the minister must be strong and creative. On the other hand, unlike many other professionals, the minister is supposed to be selfless with no desire for personal acclaim. In a world where tangible results and career accomplishments are valued more and more, ministers are haunted by the apparently decreasing social value of their work and the laity's demand that they seek no personal acclaim. In a personal way, each minister must wrestle with his or her individual priorities. Each minister must ask, "How much ambition should I have personally? How much ambition should I have for my career?"

Albert Camus in *The Fall* describes the stark image of a medieval prison. In some medieval prisons, cells were constructed in such a way that the person in one could never stretch out to full height, either standing or lying down. The individual always had to be curled up or stooped over. The authorities' hideous rationale behind this was that if the individual could never straighten up, the physical discomfort eventually would break the person's rebellious spirit.

I find this descriptive of the dilemma some ministers experience. Many ministers find that they are, by work group expectations, expected never to straighten up completely to their full height. The longer they live this way, the more lonely and hunch-backed they become. Donald P. Smith in *Clergy in the Cross Fire* quotes a study of ministers who were clients in the Midwest Career Center. Fifty-four percent of these individuals lacked "'a sense of goal-directedness'. . . . Most have 'never allowed themselves to think in terms of career goals' because this would imply that they were being 'ambitious' or were not relying on the Holy Spirit."[2]

To be certain, the minister is a "servant." Many of us have seen ambitious ministers develop negative aspects: self-aggrandizement that displaces the servant image; acceptance of success and abandonment of the prophetic task; obsessive-compulsive behavior that becomes a negative role and process model for tense, hard-driven congregants. Yet George E. Sweazy, a distinguished pastor, has written, "Clearly, ambition has no place in the Christian ministry–but the Church would be in a bad way without it."[3]

The question is a significant one. Can the minister, like other professionals, embrace personal ambition? In our seminaries we have taught, studied, and developed theologies of suffering and grace. Is there a theology of ambition and power that can accompany these well-developed theologies to protect us from passive postures in the misguided name of servanthood?

Ambition

Ministers are not exempt from human aspirations. The need for achievement is common to all professions and persons, ministry and ministers included. As George E. Sweazy has noted, ambition is a necessary goal for ministers. As a self-employed individual, the minister must have some kind of personal goal in order to maintain self-discipline. Certainly ambition is necessary for mental health in the ministry. In a profession where results are largely intangible, one must have tangible evidence of one's progress in order to find encouragement.[4]

Christ has said, "Love your neighbor as yourself." This direction implies a healthy self-love. We are called to value ourselves positively because God does. Thus there is a difference between sinful pride or arrogance and healthy Christian ambition.

Once a student, who had been actively involved in a religious group on a university campus, came into my office with some startling news. "I'm not going to finish college," he declared. "I've just been saved. I've got Jesus now, and he is all I need. He is sufficient for my every want and need. Life is easy now. I am at peace and simply take everything to God in prayer. Isn't that wonderful?"

The unfortunate aspect of this individual's experience was the negative emphasis on loving oneself and having ambitions. He had discovered Jesus, and now he was ready to wrap his personal gifts in a napkin and bury them. Such behavior was supported by inherent guilt feelings that equated any personal ambition with the sin of pride.

Likewise, one summer while on vacation I happened to worship in a church adjacent to the hotel in which I was residing. In one particular service the minister preached what I considered to be an enlightened and inspiring sermon. After the service was over, several of us visitors met her at the front door and remarked how the sermon had blessed us and challenged us. The minister replied, "I'm just grateful God spoke through me. I just prayed for God to use me. There isn't much way you can improve on Scripture."

Who preached the sermon? The minister spent many years developing the talent of preaching. And if she had not spent many hours in her study the previous week, what God said through her that morning most probably would have been superficial at best. If she had not gotten up from her bed, showered, dressed, and arrived at church before eleven o'clock, there would have been no sermon regardless of how good God is.

Somehow ministers have to recognize the point where God ends and they begin.

I personally believe that the liberation theologians have much to offer us in this regard. The words of Justo and Catherine Gonzalez are very significant for what I consider to be this "oppressed" profession of ministry.

Too often has the Reformation doctrine of justification by faith been presented in such a manner. It is significant that many of those who tell us that humility is the greatest virtue, or that the root of all sin is pride, are doing so from prestigious pulpits and endowed chairs. The tone of the Bible is very different. There the beauty of creation is used to exalt God, and the human creature is seen as the crown of that creation (Ps. 8). Nowhere does the Bible tell us that we are called to be nothing. Rather, we are told that we are made after the divine image, that we are heirs of the Kingdom, children of God, priests and royalty. Any supposed humility that denies this is sinful, for it rejects the divine plan for creation. And yet, traditional theology has often been bent on promoting the virtue of humility, particularly since those who are humble will stay in their place and refuse to claim their rightful status in human societies as children and heirs of God.[5]

Jaroslav Pelikan is one of our nation's premier church historians. In an address at Upsala College he made some observations that anticipate the posture of liberation theology, "There is perhaps no greater need in Christian thought today than the development of a theology of ambition. . . . Christian theology has had comparatively little to say about the sin of refusing to become everything that one can be. . . ."[6]

There is virtue, in my opinion, in Christian ambition, just as there is virtue in Christian humility. A minister is no less called than others to accept the possibilities God places in life. To deny all personal ambition and produce guilt in oneself over any sign of ambition is detrimental to effective Christian growth. I personally believe that God wants none of us to suppress his or her personal development.

Abraham Maslow has identified the importance of *esteem needs* and Erik Erickson has focused on *industry* versus *inferiority* in the development of persons. Certainly no minister can minister effectively without an operational theology that enables him or her to pursue adequately the fulfillment of those needs. Without a theological undergirding for personal ambition, the minister faces a crisis of power: "I know what I should do but my servanthood won't let me."

Theological Reinforcement for Ministry

The Reverend Seward Hiltner, professor of theology and personality at Princeton Theological Seminary since 1961, has written recently of the need for ministers to focus on their theological responsibility. In working with ministers enrolled in the seminary's

Doctor of Ministry program, Hiltner noted that these "generally able and talented . . . ministers had done very little to cultivate theological reflection on their actual experiences of ministry." His experience with ministers led him to articulate that ". . . most ministers have come to regard theology as a kind of magic helper, usually elusive, but capable of reinforcing one's ministry efforts if only one can hit on the correct positive note."[7]

My own work with ministers on sabbatical leave from their churches has prompted me to affirm Hiltner's findings. Most ministers have not sufficiently reflected on their daily tasks in such a way as to bring, in Hiltner's words, "to bear on a situation the most relevant theological insights."[8] In short, they lack an operational theology sufficient to provide them with the necessary theological reinforcement for ministry.

While such categories should never be absolutized, there are basically three ways of doing theology. *Dogmatic theology* deals with answers, clarifying what is true or false. It is a "public theology," what a minister says he or she believes. *Systematic theology* deals with questions. It is an intellectual theology, emphasizing the questions the theologian or minister believes are important. A third way of approaching theology is experientially. *Operational theology* deals with primary reality, with one's situation in life. It is essentially how one's belief operates in one's life. This is the theology that ministers reflect in their value systems and their life-styles. It is hoped that the operational theology matches the minister's systematic theology and dogmatic theology. When it doesn't, the systematic theology becomes what the minister wishes he or she believed and dogmatic theology become what the minister wants the public to think the minister believes.[9]

A good illustration of unmatched theology is the attitude toward church administrative tasks. The results of studies, starting with that conducted by Sam Blizzard in 1958 to those by Lyle Schaller and others in the 1970s, have agreed on how ministers perceive the importance of their ministerial roles compared to the actual allocation of their time. The results are show in the Chart on page 48.

Most ministers spend the bulk of their time doing what their systematic and dogmatic perceptions tell them they should be spending very little of their time doing. The battle to keep a theological perspective before one in such a situation must be a mighty one indeed.

Role	Order in Which Time Should Be Spent	Order in Which Time Is Actually Spent
Preacher	1	2
Pastor	2	3
Theologian	3	4
Marketer	4	6
Administrator	5	1
Traveler	6	5

Is management, or administration, in ministry a theological enterprise, or is it the exercise of a professional service? In early Christianity, the "management of the household" was initially viewed as a theological enterprise (or, in the realm of what we today would call theology). *Oikonomia* is derived from the Greek word for administration of a household; *oikos* means "house." In Pauline references (1 Corinthians 4:1 and 9:17) the work of a church leader and of the church itself is acceptance of *oikonomia*, participation in a divine plan for creation that waits "with eager longing" for fulfillment. Ephesians 1:10 speaks of God's economy or plan for the management of God's household. The word "theology" was not in general use by the church until the fifth century because of pagan connotations. *Theologia* was restricted to the understanding of the nature of God. *Oikonomia* was understood as the work of God on behalf of humanity. Thus the work aspect of theology was called *oikonomia* because this was a reflection not only of God's self-revelation in Christ but also of God's continuing work in the world. *Consequently, when we speak of administration of the household (world-church), we are speaking in the Christian tradition of a concept that has its roots deep in the early church's vision of the theological enterprise.*

Administration and management, then, are theological and not secular in origin. To the extent that a minister "manages the household" of God in enabling a community of faith to (1) establish a redemptive, caring fellowship, (2) enable the growth and empowerment of persons, (3) interpret, express, and enrich the faith of its members, and (4) reach out in mission to others, he or she is engaging in a theological enterprise. Without a doubt, the minister must not confuse the maintenance goals of the institution with the actual primary theological goals of that institution. But when a minister furthers the cause of the kingdom of God through utilizing management skills to unleash the human, material, financial, and building resources of the people who call him or her "minister," that task is decidedly a theological one.

While this has been but one illustration of a larger problem, suffice it to say that a minister must have a theological undergirding at the operational level of existence for that ministry to make sense. Unlike many other professions, the ministry demands constant reflection.

Toward a Theology of Power

The idea of power is in no way alien to Christianity. In fact, the idea of power is in no way alien to any religion. James Luther Adams has noted that, "There is no notion of God, even among primitive peoples, in which deity is not power, or does not have power."[10]

The great systematic theologian, Paul Tillich, equated power with spirit and contended that the spirit is the power of life. Tillich recognized leadership and power as the most conspicuous ambiguities of community. A community must create centeredness by forming "a ruling group which itself is represented by an individual [in this case, the minister]. In such an individual," Tillich notes, "communal centeredness is embodied in psychosomatic centeredness."[11] The minister represents the center, but the minister is not the center in the way that a person's own self is the center of his or her being.[12] And so, the idea of ministerial "power," symbolically speaking, is in no way unnecessary to the proper fulfillment of the ministerial task. In fact, James Luther Adams contends that religion itself ". . . cannot be adequately described without employing the conception of power. . . ."[13] One can make the same claim for the individual who represents the centeredness of religious groups, namely the minister.

The kingdom of God as understood by biblical writers is a dynamic power on earth that struggles with demonic forces which are as powerful in churches as in empires. Since God as the *power* of being is the source of all particular powers of being within this kingdom, "power" is divine in its essential nature.[14]

Consequently, a main function of the ministry is equipping persons and groups to live with greater power and effectiveness. The minister is one who actively engages in releasing the power potential of persons to take charge of their own lives and to develop resources and skills necessary for human liberation.

In an article entitled "Blessed Are the Powerful," James Luther Adams contends that this goal in ministry is based on the conviction that "Jesus Christ is the spearhead of the divine power, breaking into history and pointing beyond history, bringing healing to men, calling them into a new covenant of righteousness . . . that . . . formed a new universal community." This spirit of power gave birth to the early church, which was an "institutional expression precisely among people who previously had been denied opportunities to participate"[15] in making decisions that influenced their lives.

Power, in such case, is a Christian virtue. Jesus is seen as coming with power and providing his followers with a gift of power. The teachings in the Sermon on the Mount deal with the complete transformation in the balance of power as Jesus shifted power away from economic privilege and social rank toward those who seek God. Jesus, as such, was a redeemer or liberator in the sense that he freed people for self-fulfillment and self-affirmation.

Taking Charge

Edgar M. Grider has noted that the vocabulary of the minister abounds in terms referring to power. Words such as "strength," "might," and "powerful" appear in the majority of Sunday sermons.[16] Clergypersons encourage people to see themselves as persons of worth and dignity, as the "light of the world" and the "salt of the earth," capable of making a difference in the world through taking charge of their own lives. "Yet," as studies by Grider and others have indicated, "very few ministers will identify themselves with power! . . . It's as though the reality of *power* were out of place in the ministry, totally inappropriate to apply either to ministers or churches."[17]

This proclivity toward personal disassociation from power in the name of servanthood creates for the minister a "double anxiety." Psychiatrist Rollo May suggests that the dominant values of competition and success in our culture increase a basic anxiety in us all.[18] Success through competition often becomes the criterion by which our society evaluates and validates self-worth. In addition to that prevalent societal pressure, which certainly affects the minister as a participant in society, the minister places himself or herself in an impossible situation if he or she is reluctant to own and use the "power" that comes from being a minister. Ministers need to see that whenever a minister puts his or her physical, emotional, and mental capacities into operation to create occasions for others to use their abilities, that is an exercise of their power.

Robert C. Linthicum has written extensively on church renewal. He maintains, "All other factors being equal, whenever you see a church that is rapidly growing, you can bet on one thing: someone is hustling. In the final analysis, church growth today comes through hard work—contacting potential members, telling them about the church, and inviting them to a membership class, encouraging them to make a decision for the Christ and his Kingdom."[19]

Ministers are in a unique position among professionals to exercise personal power if they are willing to claim the exercise of power as an area of their lives that possesses theological undergirding. This is not to say that ministers should dilute the biblical norms into a "theology of the feasible." But it is to say that in the area of operational theology there is much to support ministers who strive for quality in their own performance of ministerial tasks.

In the ministry, as much as in any other profession, one has an opportunity to determine one's own leadership style. Since groups largely adopt the style of a leader (especially if the leader employs a collaborative style) what the minister expects from himself or herself and from others in the church is very crucial. Certainly ministers should not become workaholics or obsessive-compulsive persons out of feelings of inadequacy or overidentification with God; yet when ministers set low goals or tolerate indifferent responses from lay people, they exercise a mediocre style that can cripple the vitality of a community of faith. Mediocrity is an infectious disease. If a minister tolerates mediocrity in himself or herself, soon the lay members will be setting low goals for themselves and their church and thereby expect little in the way of performance from their church. In like manner, the minister who tolerates mediocrity in church members develops an equal tendency to tolerate it in himself or herself.

Ministers must do more than minister to persons' needs. Ministers must also equip persons for ministry. If the church's ministry is limited to what the minister can do, that minister is a *doer* and not a *leader*. Further, when he or she leaves the parish, a sinking hulk is left behind. Remember, your style is both to serve and to equip. If you become reactive, you lose intentionality and soon become exhausted spiritually and mentally.

I personally believe that ministers should set high goals for themselves and their congregants and not feel guilty if personal acclaim results from their work. The minister is both a servant and a professional who exercises "power" in the utilization of talents and skills. Personal ambition, contrary to implications that one is not relying enough on the Holy Spirit, may actually be an acceptance of the Holy Spirit itself.

Power and Ambition Beyond the Church

John P. Kildahl, a clinical psychologist, contends that a minister is in sad shape if the minister's "religion . . . [tends] to become virtually his *sole* source of [personal] gratification." After identifying five elemental emotional needs—"1) a feeling of self-esteem . . .; 2) . . . being able to cope with one's environment; 3) meaningful interpersonal relationships; 4) satisfaction of physical functions . . .; and 5) a unifying view of life that gives coherence and direction to one's existence"—Kildahl posits that the minister "should make sure that his nonprofessional life is so satisfying that he need not use the church's activities or people as a means for gaining his sense of well-being." In short, the minister "should have nonprofessional activities and relationships which supply the inevitable needs he has for self-respect, success, and personal dignity."[20]

The minister should feel that he or she is a successful person even when a bad sermon is occasionally preached or a layman is sorely offended by some church action. If the minister's "self-esteem rises and falls with the climate of the church council meeting, then the minister will lack the freedom necessary to do a creative task."[21]

The majority of successful ministers I know are individuals who find satisfaction in activities or part-time jobs outside the church as semi-professional photographers, real estate brokers, authors, and civic leaders. They bring to their work of the ministry a vigor and objectivity that free the best of their own potentialities.

I am amazed at how many ministers lack what Wayne Oates calls "ventilating relationships." Without opportunities to participate in friendships and share mutually stimulating insights with members of other professions, ministers become very one-dimensional people. Quite often a minister "talks only to religious people, attends only religious conferences, and hears only religious language until he is breathing the same old air over and over."[22]

When I asked respondents to my survey to "describe your three closest friends, how long you have known them, and in what capacity," only 51 (38 percent) of the 134 friends listed were members of other professions. And perhaps even more amazing, 51 percent of the total friends listed were other religious professionals. A forty-eight-year-old minister with twenty-two years of experience in the ministry said that the least attractive feature of the ministry for him was "the stagnant, stale members of the clergy with whom I work."

I firmly believe that ministers should use some of their continuing education time and energies pursuing studies and projects outside their own profession. In my Massachusetts study are hung, side by side, two plaques that mean much to me. The first is a resolution from the Trinity Baptist Church, Seneca, South Carolina, commending the ministry I had as pastor among that congregation. The second plaque is a similar resolution from the Judge of the Oconee County Family Court signed by the members of the Commission on Alcohol and Drug Abuse. I chaired the Commission during its initial establishment as an agency. To be certain, the latter plaque represents an evening a week away from family and church, two weeks in Miami in a program sponsored by a medical school, much hard study, and weeks of visiting centers in other cities and towns. But the self-esteem and personal accomplishment derived from the "nonprofessional" participation made ministry a much more objective phenomenon for me.

Continued education in another field would help to eliminate some of the problem areas in ministry. The work area in ministry which is least attractive to the fifty respondents in my survey is administration. Thirty-one of these ministers, or 62 percent, listed aspects of administration, such as time management and office detail, as the least attractive features of the ministry for them.

Yet in the four years I have assisted clergy plan their sabbatical studies, I have had only one minister take advantage of the opportunity to study (free of charge!) in the Harvard Business School. In fact, when I began to prepare to teach a course on parish development and management, I sought the assistance of three colleagues on the faculty of Harvard Business School. These colleagues, all members of Boston area churches, informed me that they had *never* had a minister in one of their courses. Nor had any minister approached them privately about readings or study in administrative planning.

Likewise, when I taught a course in management in Union Theological Seminary in Richmond, Virginia, ministers appeared more interested in abstract theological matters than in a theology of management in terms of their academic background. Their theology did not undergird their practical ministry. During one session of the course, Peter Trost, of Chesapeake Container Corporation in Richmond, visited the class. He told us that while he manages employees, almost all of whom belong to area churches, not a single minister has visited his facility or ever talked with him, asking advice on management or administration. He indicated that he would have freely assisted such ministers in improving their administrative skills.

When I think of the number of doctors, lawyers, and corporate personnel managers who sought my advice on counseling and understanding the religious and personal needs of employees, I wonder why ministers as a whole have not made the acquisition of extraprofessional skills a two-way street.

Certainly the ministry itself cannot bear the total weight of personal fulfillment. A thirty-two-year-old minister with seven years' experience in ministry responded to the question in my survey about the least attractive feature in ministry with these words:

> It's the lack of intellectual stimulation. The job rarely calls on me to use the skills of conceptualizing, thinking analytically, researching, and trying to break new intellectual ground—skills which I honed in graduate school and which make use of my best talents.

I'm not certain that the gratification necessary to eliminate that desire will ever be found within pastoral community. If the church and its members are virtually the sole source of personal gratification, the job is carrying a larger burden than it should have to bear.

4

Loneliness Is a
Faith Issue

It is my belief that when people do not feel that their work is understood, valued, and supported as purposeful by their work group, they become overly concerned with their adequacy as persons. This idea is borne out in studies of clergy. The Menninger Foundation recently conducted a study of 140 ministers and diagnosed 33 of them as obsessive-compulsive. An expert in time management, Speed Leas, has stated that half of all clergy work more than ten hours per day and that clergy as a profession are so consumed with their own work and own sense of importance that they suffer severe problems with compulsive working.[1] The same problem was underscored by John Harris of the Alban Institute in his book *Stress, Power and Ministry*.[2]

Spiritual Resources Needed

The ministry is a profession that demands that its members draw on available resources to affirm that their work is purposeful. Aside from informing their work group of their activities, ministers must acknowledge that for all that they do in ministry, their total affirmation will never come from other human beings. It is almost trite to say that purposeful activity in the sight of God radically differs from purposeful activity in the sight of secular society, but it is true! All of the clergy's resources against loneliness do not lie in the area of better public understanding of their function, although admittedly that would help. Spiritual resources are a crucial element in dealing with the many and varied pressures on the modern minister.

Certain cultural crises help to produce corresponding spiritual crises. Such things as Watergate, Vietnam, inflation and recession, and the energy and nuclear crises all bring spiritual questions to the forefront. The entire culture is experiencing a questioning of the purposefulness of its activities.

Clergy are impacted by these cultural shifts. Information gathered from both the media and lay assessment supports the existence of these spiritual crises in the lives of ministers. Ministers, like lay persons, must deal with their spiritual problems.

The modern day minister, however, is hardly the first to experience spiritual crises and a certain reluctance to accept the spiritual burdens of a vocation that is not understood and is sometimes hardly affirmed by one's work group. In fact, the legacy of the faith, from Moses to Jeremiah to Isaiah to Jesus, is that of wrestling with these same issues. In their anguish and loneliness, ministers have available to them the same resources of the meditative life as did their progenitors in the faith. They must have the firm conviction that they are "called"; that is, that they are urged and compelled to share what they have tasted, to improve the opportunities of others to savor that life, and to preserve what is of value within their inheritance. They are prayerful people whose goals must not become professionalized in the sense that law and medicine have become professionalized.

Unfortunately recognition of these resources does not always loom in one's consciousness in stressful times. The study on stress in the ministry by Mills and Koval in the 1970s found that almost "two-thirds of the stress periods were met with independent efforts to master the problems. . . . Religious steps [were] in low proportion compared to self-steps. . . ."[3]

In my study of fifty clergypersons, a high percentage (34 percent) indicated that they were somewhat or totally unsatisfied with the quality of their devotional lives. In fact, more of these clergy are unsatisfied with their devotional lives than with their salaries, the category that received the next highest negative response (28 percent). Yet 81 percent of these same clergy indicate that they are somewhat or totally satisfied with the freedom they have to develop their own life-styles. One cannot but conclude that the freedom to develop a devotional life-style certainly exists in the ministry, but that knowledge in how to develop it is lacking. Or, perhaps ministers are unwilling to admit the existence of their religious problems.

The Reverend Bobbie McKay, Ph.D., is a registered psychologist in Winnetka, Illinois. In her work with clients who are ministers, she has found that many ministers have expectations that they can operate in a super-human manner; this expectation does not allow for any kind of faith crisis.

While the material and spiritual dimensions of life are integrally related, in recent years the material side of ministry has become a more acute issue since the expectations of clergy have risen while membership in many Protestant denominations has declined, rising costs and inflation have become realities in our culture,[4] and ministers have become more career oriented.

Yet I believe that the findings in the *Stress in the Ministry* survey by Mills and Koval still remain operative:

> Serious morale problems exist in relation to money . . . Even more serious, however, are doubts about the worthwhileness of the parish ministry. It seems obvious that even the finest support systems and educational opportunities cannot sustain the clergyman who feels the whole enterprise is futile and ineffectual.[5]

To focus on understanding ambition and management and to advocate better financial benefits for clergy would only scratch the surface in getting at the root problems of ministerial loneliness. Certain factors in ministerial experience make it difficult for ministers to maintain the kind of spiritual life which gives value and understanding to the enterprise called "ministry."

Spirituality and Theology

Most ministers, of course, understand that there is a distinction between faith and theology. The feeling of losing one's faith while one continues to lead a sacred institution of the faith and discuss the sacred materials of the faith has always been a dangerous hazard in professional ministry. Many ministers have found that they cannot come to God with borrowed crutches—the theological supports that they have inherited from mentors or adopted from seminary professors. Crises in spirituality happen to the best of clergy. Jesus Christ himself at times had to experience solitude so that he could emerge empowered with a sense of vocation. During his earthly ministry at crucial periods he continued to withdraw from others in order to be alone and pray.

The issue of ministerial spirituality is anything but simple. Tilden Edwards, a contemporary expert on spirituality has observed at least two major impediments in the spiritual lives of ministers. The first is a problem with *the practical nature of clergy training.* Faith and prayer are seen as useful instruments in particular practical situations. "Coping with people and institutions are the valued focus. These take a lot of practical know-how."[6] Consequently prayer and faith become means to other goals in the lives of ministers rather than ends in themselves. Unfortunately, I am afraid that the same holds true in the larger church situation today.

Another major impediment to spiritual development among ministers has been the *rise of psychological schools of understanding.* Human development has been separated from its older roots in theological and ethical concern. In many instances this has been helpful, but certain blind spots have occurred and have been harmful.[7] For example, clinical pastoral education began in pathology. It attempts to uncover the pathologies inherent in the "living human documents" with which it works. Yet not every human being is encased in pathology. One of the crying needs in our time is for pastoral education that begins with the premise of normalcy within the "living human documents" with which it works. Yet religious leaders in the church have been almost totally dependent on secular models of human growth.

The separation of psychological and spiritual development from each other has actually hampered the development of theology in our time. Douglas V. Steere, the professor of philosophy at Haverford College, maintains in his writings that truly great Christian theology needs to spring from a watershed of devotion. Especially today as women's consciousness calls us to reinterpret theology and ministry from a feminist perspective, I find it notable that the theology written by persons like Dorothy Soelle, Beverly Harrison, Rosemary Reuther, Peggy Way, and others emanates from people of devotional emphasis and concern.

The same holds true for the legacy of social action which we have inherited from modern day prophets like Harry Emerson Fosdick, Walter Rauschenbusch, Martin Luther King, Jr., and Mother Theresa. These and others like them are as noted for their understanding of prayer and spirituality as they are for their social pronouncements and actions. Matthew Fox speaks of a life that is prophetically directed as possessing a "prophetic spirituality."[8]

Indeed, prophetic ministry *demands* a spiritual undergirding. Henri Bergson gets to the heart of the matter when he says in *Two Sources of Morality and Religion:*

> Mankind lies groaning half crushed beneath the weight of his own progress. . . . Now in the body distended out of all proportion, the soul remains what it was, too small to fill it, too weak to guide it. Hence the gap between the two. Hence the tremendous social, political and international problems which are just so many definitions of this gap, and which provoke so many chaotic and ineffectual efforts to fill it . . . the body now larger, calls for a bigger soul. . . .[9]

All of the stress and pressures in ministry, which I have attempted to lay bare in preceding chapters, have created a larger weight to carry. The lack of understanding of the work by the laity, conflicting expectations between parishioners and professionals, the increased total availability of the minister—these and other modern day pressures and joys have created a larger responsibility for the minister. What is needed is a bigger soul!

Practical Steps Toward Spiritual Growth

As I begin this section on practical guides for a more devout life, I want to remind the reader of my firm insistence that the ministry should not become an individual's sole source of emotional security. I still affirm nonprofessional endeavors so that a failure in one's work does not become a personal failure. Consequently I do not advocate ministers eating, breathing, and sleeping "religion." Devotional time should not become one of so many trophies on one's personal shelf.

If we are to function effectively in the ministry, we must become exposed to ways of letting go rather than ways of taking on. Many persons have become exposed to such ways through the assistance of a *spiritual guide* or *spiritual friend.*

Spiritual Guides

Spiritual guides are, of course, a part of our faith tradition.

They were present in the lives of the early Desert Fathers and Mothers to help them in their interior journeys. A negative byproduct of the Protestant Reformation has been the relative absence of "soul friends" or spiritual guides in Protestant life. As a part of the heritage of the Reformation, we have each become our own priests instead of priests to one another. I can well remember my Baptist childhood when at youth camp I was supposed to observe a "devotional quiet time" each morning. This meant sitting out under a pine tree for thirty minutes with my Bible and a passage of Scripture upon which I was supposed to reflect.

At present there is a mood among Protestants that the recovery of spirituality in our time should not concentrate on such solitary efforts. Even though the idea of having a "spiritual" or "soul" friend has not been cultivated in recent years, the time to re-embrace this concept may be upon us.

In my survey of fifty ministers, I asked this question, "When you experience religious problems, with whom do you talk?" Eleven of the respondents answered, "No one." Another twelve answered, "my wife" or "my husband." (Women ministers responding to the survey indicated the same essential patterns as male ministers on this issue.) The responses of these ministers are summed up in the words from a thirty-nine-year-old male minister with nine years' experience in the ministry, "But by and large I have never shared a problem with any peer in the ministry or with any member of my parish."

While the absence of "spiritual friends" in itself is lamentable, the fact that so many ministers are depending primarily on their spouses to carry their religious development is also fraught with dangers. A deep spiritual friendship with one's spouse is good, even desirable, for the minister. On the other hand, it would be most helpful if ministers had a spiritual friend or guide outside the marriage. Then, undiverted by possible negative and stressful dimensions of the marital relationship, the minister and the friend could reflect in ways beneficial to the marriage.[10] The fact that over 50 percent of the ministers I surveyed are either talking to no one or unloading their religious problems solely on their spouses disturbs me.

Certainly all ministers need a friend who can help them sort out the options and discern the threads woven by the Spirit of God moving in their lives. Tilden Edwards in his book *Spiritual Friend* elaborates on the qualities of a good spiritual friend. Among these qualities are experience, personal spiritual commitment, knowledge and humility, an active discipline of prayer/meditation and the capacity to be caring, sensitive, open, and flexible with another person. Edwards also provides suggestions for developing a covenant with a spiritual friend, including discussion of the content of meetings with the friend and the focus of such meetings.[11] Most clergypersons are conditioned to read Scripture very analytically. They search for the meaning of Scripture and apply it to life and historical situations. Works such as Edwards' *Spiritual Friend* and *Living Simply Through the Day*, Kenneth Leech's *Soul Friend*, and Douglas V. Steere's *On Beginning from Within* can help the minister to use Scripture devotionally.

Having said all this, I imagine that the presence of some spiritual friend in the lives of most ministers has been an important, although not consciously recognized, part of their ministry. My own spiritual friend has been an elderly woman in the first church I pastored. At the time we began our relationship, she was sixty-nine years old. She served as guide and "Mother Confessor" to me and another minister, a forty-five-year-old in another denomination. My frequent visits to her taught me much about meditation, devotion, and prayer. It was a source of great comfort to know that another human being, outside of my family, cared greatly for my soul's development. It made me feel a little less alone in my search for spiritual growth. In addition, the regular nature of my visits brought a kind of accountability to my devotional life that was very important. To this very day, my spiritual friend and I write at least once a month even though many hundreds of miles separate us. To do less would violate the covenant between us.

I will not be so expansive or pretentious as to elaborate here on the many aspects of devotional life available to the minister. That is not the purpose of this book. Books on prayer and meditation abound. I simply want to assert that any minister who seeks to minister effectively must build a regular devotional time into his or her busy life. Spiritual resources must not be neglected in the attempts to manage a minister's sense of personal and professional loneliness.

Journals

While there is little literature on the process of journal keeping, I believe that the minister who strives to keep a personal journal greatly enhances his or her spiritual life. The personal journal can be a responsible tool for personal growth. Perhaps the most instructive resource for maintaining a personal journal is the work by George F. Simons, *Keeping Your Personal Journal*.

In my own ministry I seek to preserve thirty minutes at least two days per week to keep my religious diary. Ideally, I would like to write in my journal every day of the week. The religious journal is not so much keeping a diary of events as it is writing down one's perception of one's own religious situation. Here one records things that one does not say elsewhere.

As Simons has noted, "What goes into your [personal religious] journal [depends upon] the purpose for which you keep a journal in the first place." There are no "clean cut" rules that decide the content of the journal.[12] My own efforts have been focused on assembling the bits and pieces of my life that seem promising or problematic. I conclude each entry or description of an event or experience with a little written prayer for myself in that situation.

The minister's journal, of course, should become a matter of personal growth and spiritual discipline, not an added burden in an already busy schedule. It should never become a duty that precipitates guilt when neglected—some times in life seem more conducive to writing than other times. Nor should a personal religious journal be merely a chronicle of job satisfactions, accomplishments, problems, and noteworthy vocational happenings.

It should, at the very least, assist a minister in the effort to discern the relationship between *production* and *reproduction* in life. Many times in life we concentrate on our productive sphere and not on the reproductive sphere, which encompasses our health, our personal faith pilgrimage, and our family relationships. A well-kept and carefully reflected upon personal journal can help us attain greater freedom and insight as we decide how to place our own and others' priorities on our inner agenda.

George F. Simons lists some topics that prove particularly provocative in journal writing:

- People—in your past, present, future.
- Your job, hobbies, skills, career.
- Your body or any part of it.
- Dream and fantasy figures.
- Important moments and events, both personal and public.

- Literary, historical, artistic, or religious works, persons, events, or places.
- Feelings, e.g., anger, joy, pain, boredom, fear, emptiness.[13]
- Unfinished decisions, plans.

Milt Hughes in his *Spiritual Journey Notebook*[14] offers a workbook designed to provide a direct incentive to do Bible and other religious reading and study. Special pages facilitate study of the Bible and other books as well as keeping track of prayer concerns.

Whatever the method, journal keeping has been a rich experience for many ministers because of its personal and autonomous quality. I have certainly found that it provides me with an instrument with which to reflect theologically on the way God has been revealed through my life and through my work with people. I am afraid that without that instrument my projected future (the huge vocational agenda I have for myself and for society in general) would erode the potency of my present existence. I have found, as have many other ministers, that I must have practical measures to help me keep my destructive tendencies in check.

Part Two

The Minister's Relationship with the Congregation

5

The Burden of Prophetic Compassion

Role conflict occurs when two or more role expectations interfere with each other or contradict one another altogether. (Donald P. Smith)[1]

Among the various professions the ministry is probably the one which most often seems to place its practitioners squarely on the intersection of comfort and confrontation. Few other professions by their historical calling are expected to run the flags of both personal regeneration and prophetic proclamation up the flagpole. The ministry by its very nature demands that the minister strive to see that social concern, which was so prevalent in our culture in the 1960s, and personal concern, which dominated the 1970s, are held together as two sides of one reality, the gospel of Jesus Christ. More than one minister has recognized that these role expectations interfere with each other and appear at times to contradict each other. Yet all recognize the chaos that would result in community life and the distortions of the gospel that would appear should the minister place both feet squarely in one role or the other.

Philip Brooks is reported to have said that one must be both a preacher and a pastor; a preacher who isn't a pastor tends to be irrelevant and a pastor who isn't a preacher tends to get petty. I agree with Brooks that the minister is to be a prophet who comforts and a comforter who prophesizes. Certainly most modern day clergy have accepted the task that Dr. Ralph W. Sockman stated: "It is my

67

business to comfort the afflicted and afflict the comfortable."[2]

That may indeed be the business of ministry. But it is hard, and it's getting harder. The extensive studies that have been conducted on conflicts among external expectations in the ministry in the past twenty years point to

> The basic lines of conflict . . . as drawn between a social challenge to change, on the one hand, and personal comfort or reassurance in the midst of life's vicissitudes on the other; between the church as an agent of change in the world and the church as a haven from change; between involvement in social-political-economic issues and concentration upon personal religion.[3]

My own research among fifty ministers shows that this conflict is still one of the dominant frustrations in ministry. The second most frequent response (20 percent of the respondents placed it first) to the question about the least attractive feature in ministry was precisely this conflict. Two ministers summed up the frustration:

> The least attractive feature of the ministry is being patient and loving with Christians who mesh their not yet sanctified actions and attitudes under more noble guises. Since I am not yet perfect, it is hard to be patient and loving without becoming a doormat. (thirty-four-year-old female with eight years in the ministry.)
>
> I find myself well able to achieve relatively high levels of congregational support and approval for what I do—but I also am concerned that such congregational support and approval may detract from some of the tough demands of the gospel in a world of shrinking resources and expanding expectations. I am concerned about the above discrepancy because I find my life needs deeper and stronger meaning than the approval of others. (forty-two-year-old male minister with seventeen years' experience in the ministry.)

The dilemma, of course, is not necessarily clarified or resolved by attempts to identify with the life of Jesus of Nazareth. Divergent interpretations of his life add confusion rather than clarity. Robert Pfeiffer points out:

> He is said to have been a prophet; the Davidic Messiah; the angelic Son of Man, . . . coming at the end of time to judge the quick and the dead; the Lord . . . who conferred regeneration and eternal life through his death; the incarnate Logos (Word) through whom God created the world; and the Son of God. The simplest, truest . . . statement is that of Peter: Jesus went about doing good (Acts 10:38).[4]

And when we look to Jesus' personality as a prototype for the modern minister's attempt to serve as a guide to both societal and personal reconstruction, we see an impossible series of contrasts presented in Scripture. Jesus was "a proud lord and a humble servant, a king and a beggar, a dominating personality, and a childlike spirit, an upholder and a demolisher of the Law of Moses; a violent fighter—and yet meek and lowly of heart, . . ."[5] Perhaps the pertinent question is, "With which Jesus do I identify?"

To approach an understanding of the prophetic-therapeutic tension, one must, of course, set Jesus within the prophetic stream of consciousness which predated him. One must also acknowledge one's own prejudices that are brought to this "backward glance."

Harrison Peyton, who has been an effective local minister for over twenty-seven years, has provided some helpful insights into effective preaching. His view is that community must be established before effective prophetic preaching can be done. A community must be created in which tensions from disagreements can be dealt with in a creative way. The foundation of this community is grace. Regardless of the techniques used in prophetic preaching and therapeutic counseling, the bottom line is still grace. Without an environment in which individuals can be accepted and doors opened up for new growth, prophecy indeed becomes irrelevant and counseling becomes petty.

Peton has also provided me with some helpful insights into ways to establish this "community of grace": 1) The preacher must be a *listener* who values the opinions of others. 2) The preacher must recognize the partial nature of his or her truth. All the resources of faith and experience are distilled through persons' minds and personalities. No minister can possibly proclaim *the truth*. Truth may be *the truth* for a particular person, but he or she does not own all of truth. Consequently, ministers must work through changes with their congregations when they have changed their minds about some things. 3) Preachers must respond to human need regardless of a person's posture toward the preacher as a proclaimer. A minister has to *earn* the right of proclamation.[6]

The modern day ministers, try as we might, cannot separate ourselves from the "royal consciousness" of which we are a part. To a certain degree, our access to God and our proclamation of that access are controlled by the culture that maintains us. Perhaps the proper question for us is not how do we become prophets in the true sense of the word, but how do we, who are a part of the royal consciousness, embrace prophetic alternatives? How do we bring to public expression the very hopes that the institutionalization of our profession tends to deny and even repress?

Allow me to illustrate this dilemma from personal experience. The voters in Massachusetts passed a proposition that reduced the revenues generated from local property taxes. This measure reduced the funds available for public education. This, coupled with the shrinking number of elementary school children, necessitated making some hard decisions about closing some neighborhood schools. Many of us parents met late into the evenings to discuss the lamentable situation. During one particular meeting, a local minister came and remarked, "I feel compelled to stand as a prophet in this situation." He implied that his very presence there was symbolic of a prophetic act.

His posture upset me for several reasons. In the first place, he lived in a parsonage and paid no property taxes. While the rest of us were paying several thousand dollars each per year to support the schools and town government, the tax laws of the country protected him and his house. The "royal consciousness," dictated that he pay nothing. In addition, the business that employed him, the church, paid no taxes, unlike the other businesses represented in the meeting. In fact, one of the reasons for the high taxation was the fact that so much of the property in town was religious in nature—parsonages, church buildings, church cemeteries.

My contention was that this gentleman could utter a prophetic word in our midst or at best suggest to us some prophetic alternatives. But as one protected by the royal consciousness of the culture, he could not claim to be "the prophet" in our midst.

I contend that prophecy in its purest form from a base in a local church is difficult if not impossible. The activity of the Old Testament prophets and of Jesus himself was possible only because of a peculiar aspect of the social organization of the society in which they were placed. The prophets and Jesus could not have emerged as they did had they not been able to appeal directly to the people. As *indirect* appealers to the people who choose to enter our doors (as persons who are to some extent standing under an institutional umbrella), our prophetic proclamations are at best suggestions of prophetic alternatives.

Consequently, the task of prophetic speaking is perhaps best stated in the words of Walter Brueggemann in his salient work, *The Prophetic Imagination: "The task of prophetic ministry is to nurture, nourish, and evoke a consciousness and perception alternative to the consciousness and perception of the dominant culture around us."*[7] As to exactly how one evokes this consciousness and perception, one must turn to the elements of prophecy as expressed in our Scriptural prophetic heritage.

The Elements of Prophetic Preaching

As members of an institution called the church, which exists to energize religious memories and radical hopes, ministers, in my opinion, must remember that the characteristic idiom of prophetic preaching is not anger but anguish. The contemporary American church is strongly culturally influenced by the American ethos of consumerism. This is true of both its liberal and conservative expressions. Yet from Hosea to Jeremiah to Jesus, the prophet has been one who expressed solidarity with the marginal people in society (lepers, shepherds, women). The prophet had been the one who brought to public expression the suffering and grief the royal culture tried to suppress. Nevertheless, the manner in which Jesus of Nazareth brought this consciousness to public expression was in the language of anguish.[8] Given the realities of contemporary ministry, it seems appropriate to keep this expression in mind when attempting to effect prophetic change.

J. Alfred Smith, a forceful black pastor in Oakland, California, tells a story that graphically illustrates this point.[9] It seems that a particular church in a hierarchical denomination had become well known as a graveyard for ministers. The internal conflicts of the church usually resulted in requests to transfer the pastors after but a brief residence. A new bishop arrived on the scene and immediately sent to this church one of the brightest and apparently most capable ministers in the district. True to form, within a year the chairperson of the personnel committee called the Bishop and informed him that the church wanted the minister moved on to another setting. "What's the problem?" asked the Bishop. "Well," came the reply, "all he does is get up every Sunday and tell us all that we're going to hell."

Reluctantly the Bishop arranged for the transfer of the minister to another church. This time he sent a much older person to be the minister of the church and settled back in partial contentment that he had eliminated one of his headache churches. But, alas, within six months the chairperson of the personnel committee was back on the phone to the Bishop, "This preacher's no better than the rest of them. All he does is get up every Sunday and tell us all that we're going to hell."

Totally exasperated, the Bishop decided to fight fire with fire. He sent into the church an aggressive, young, recent seminary graduate who had been well known in seminary for championing every social cause from abortion to draft evasion. The Bishop grimly dug in his heels and waited for the thunder and lightning to strike. But three and a half years passed and he never heard a word. The annual reports indicated that the congregation had grown substantially in attendance and budget and had even embarked on a few new social programs. The Bishop's curiosity peaked and he called the chairperson of the church's personnel committee. "How do you like your minister?" he asked. "He's wonderful," came the reply. "I don't get it," said the Bishop. "I thought that certainly this minister would prophetically tell you that you're going to hell if you don't change your ways."

"Oh," said the layperson, "hardly a Sunday passes that our minister doesn't tell us we're going to hell. *But he cries about it.*"

The characteristic idiom of the prophet is not anger but anguish. Rather than mechanically denouncing wrong actions, the true prophet treats each situation sensitively. Further, the true prophet is not speaking from outside the situation but rather from within it.

Another element of prophecy is *denouncement of nationalistic renderings about God.* Dispelling the concept of God as a benefactor deity is a prophetic concern. As the prophetic minister champions an openness to history, he or she evidences a profound critique of the concept of a partisan God and encourages awe of an ethically exalted God as a motivation against nationalism.

Nationalistic renderings of God follow a rather clear evolutionary pattern in the history of Israelite prophecy. The ninth century B.C. prophets showed belief in a benefactor and partisan deity. These prophets supported and even directed kings in their wars against foreign powers as the prophets witnessed the encroachment of Baal in Israel and among its enemies. For these prophets *"international relations ... meant largely either the sphere of Yahweh's effective power in enforcing the rule of Israel or the sphere of subtle and disastrous temptation to religious syncretism and compromise."*[10]

While the concept of foreign powers as instruments of Yahweh's punishment was not dominant in these ninth century B.C. traditions, it began to dominate the Deuteronomic outlook where Yahweh was viewed as one who dominates history as a whole. And by the time of Amos, a broader international context for Yahweh became determinative for the prophet.[11] In fact, Amos placed ". . . the whole family which I [Yahweh] brought up out of the land of Egypt . . ." among "all the families of the earth . . ." (Amos 3:1-2). Thus the big issue that confronted Israelite prophecy was the issue as to whether Israel was unique or like other nations. In short, were other nations in existence solely for punishment of Israel or did they have intrinsic significance for Yahweh and for Yahweh's prophet? Norman Gottwald, Old Testament scholar, concludes that Amos succeeded *"in establishing both Israel's importance as a unique people and her merely proximate importance to a God for whom all peoples count and who possesses many resources for bringing justice to earth."*[12]

This resolution of the "prophetic dilemma" continued in the works of Hosea and Isaiah of Jerusalem. Hosea contended that a nation cannot excuse its political sins by blaming them on the enemy while Isaiah of Jerusalem raised the motif of Yahweh as the judge of all national prides. As such, Isaiah attempted for the first time on a broad basis to deal with foreign nations as realities in their own right.[13]

Consequently, the modern preacher who needs to transmit a prophetic message must remember that the prophets in general regarded political institutions, especially sovereign states, merely as instruments in the plan of God. These institutions did not have final values. Obviously, this demands that the minister view the United States of America in ways conflicting with the views of many parishioners. To identify the will of God solely with the destiny of the United States would not be within the prophetic continuum. Thus the minister is called to establish the United States' importance as a unique and blessed nation and its "merely proximate importance to a God for whom all peoples count."

A third crucial component in prophetic preaching is the *concept of communal responsibility*. The examination of the origin and impetus of corporate responsibility in the Judeo-Christian heritage is itself a relatively recent enterprise so that our construction of this concept cannot be as tenable as it might deserve to be. Only from the eighth century B.C. can we assert that the idea of indicting the whole nation for the actions of its leaders has been a vital part of prophetic consciousness.[14] Salvation, coming in the shadow of judgment, is offered to the corporate personality or the ongoing community. There is a corporate responsibility laden on the universal church by its prophetic heritage.

The Israelite prophets constantly oscillated between speaking to individuals and to the groups to which the individuals belonged. A representative figure in many instances was said to embody the group or in other instances the group was said to sum up the host of individuals. For example, the national history could be described through the life-story of an unchaste woman (Ezekiel 6:8-9 and 23:1-49) or through a forsaken and barren but now restored wife and mother of many children (Isaiah 54:1-17).

There never was a sharp antithesis between the individual and society in prophetic thought. Nor is there one today. The individual comes into existence through some form of society and depends upon it for growth. Conversely, the society finds expression only through the individuals who compose it. But, as H. Wheeler Robinson has noted, while there was consciousness of the individual in the early periods of Israel's history, the individual then was more conscious of being one of the group than individuals are today.[15]

Consequently, both the responsibility and the need exist for the modern day minister to preach an ethic that is not individualistic but communal. The championing of various social causes such as a sound economy, good government, racial equality, and women's rights, stems from a critique of prevailing culture and a strong concept of corporate responsibility. Communities as well as individuals are responsible for sin. Liberation theologians are correct in asking us why it is that in so much preaching and teaching in the church sin is usually associated with an inner attitude or private misdeeds and so seldom with the type of sin most often condemned in the Bible.

A fourth component in prophetic preaching is *the objectivity of the spoken word*. A prophet understands the distinctive power of language. The Word of God, once spoken through a prophet, becomes liberated so that it is "powerful far beyond the personal range of the prophet's activity. Once spoken . . . [the] word . . . enters upon its own independent history."[16] In short, the word is authenticated not by the life of the speaker but by its own inherent worth. Samuel Miller, in the zenith period of Harry Emerson Fosdick's ministry, made this salient observation: "The dynamic is not so much in him as in the thing of which he speaks."[17]

The Israelite prophets, of course, subscribed to the religious idea that there is a purpose in the midst of the flux of history. As Norman Gottwald has observed, they believed that the plan of God *"possesses a unity beyond human comprehension, for the parts visible to any one man at any one time are often strangely and bafflingly inconsistent."*[18] This conception of history as a unity, derived from the Hebrew prophets, not only affirms that the present word is objective, entering into its own independent history that provides a continuum into the future, but also enables the prophet to interpret past, present, and future.

A fifth component in prophetic preaching is precisely this interpretation of past, present, and future. Perhaps the greatest contribution classical prophecy rendered to the Israelite heritage was the unleashing of a forward movement.[19] Prophecy contributed to the ethical validity of Israel's mission by calling for response and decision and by relating present to future in terms of the historic purpose of God and God's moral government of the world. A prophet, then, may describe things as already carried out.

Another essential requisite for a prophetic consciousness is *the recognition that a more complex civilization is not necessarily a higher form of life.* The prophetic preacher pleads for the recognition of the instability of a human-centered society.[20] The prophetic minister is placed within this consciousness and speaks against belief in inevitable progress. Insisting, though subtly, on the reality of sin, the minister critiques the doctrine of progress. This heritage stems from the mode of expression used by the Israelite prophets. The prophets of Israel expressed their political concern by using "old" Israelite religious motifs and literary forms.

A final component which I wish to ascribe to prophetic consciousness is the *use of secular language to interpret God.* This stems from the prophetic concept of revelation as human experience. The prophet is one who takes the best insights of all theological, political, and psychological trends and substitutes them for the traditional God language. Social forces, comparative religious and experiential values all hold places in the religious vocabulary of prophetic preaching.

In summary a minister who embraces prophetic alternatives uses the language of anguish, stresses faith as an openness to history, attacks the concept of God as a benefactor deity, embraces the concept of corporate responsibility, has his or her word authenticated by its inherent worth, interprets the past, present, and future, critiques the doctrine of inevitable progress, and uses secular language to depict God.

Therapy and Prophecy: A Mediating Position

It is my conviction that prophecy is a form of therapy. A minister who is concerned about the individual lives of parishioners knows that prophecy and counseling are two sides of a larger reality. The key to solving what may appear to be an impasse—how to be both prophetic and therapeutic—for me lies in the distinction between *integration* and *integrity*. Appeals to individuals for self-integration and self-acceptance which lack an ethical base do not harness the religious dynamic. Lives can be *integrated* at low levels. If an individual emerges from the church psychologically well (integrated) and at the same time ethically dangerous, very little has been accomplished for the kingdom of God. On the other hand, a sense of integrity does not demand that the prophetic minister devote an entire sermon to denunciation of the ethics of a social or economic question. A community of grace does not resort to direct assault but favors a more balanced denunciation of social problems.

Psychology is a very effective entreé into prophecy. Ethics and psychology can sharpen the awareness of each other, when the minister displays acquaintance with depth psychology's understanding of forgiveness and reconciliation while taking the biblical concept of sin most seriously. This mediation takes place when the minister realizes that the individual is not separable from his or her social environment, able to do what he or she will with life. Indeed, personality is a social product. Personal life can grow only in the matrix of social relationships.

Religious experience is composed of two attributes: a self-commitment to something greater than one's own personal interests and a transforming inward sense of peace and unity. Such experience cuts across easy dichotomies between counseling and proclaiming, comforting and challenging, conservative and liberal. The minister proclaims a God of both undying love *and* moral judgment. Thus the Christian faith is both medicine to be prescribed and a gospel to be proclaimed. Individuals whose lives are psychologically integrated but ethically sick are victimizers in our social order. Yet individuals must be free from their own self-absorbing hang-ups to be spontaneously concerned about others. The Christian gospel is a very heavy two-edged sword.

Consequently, I think the term "counseling" is perhaps an inadequate categorization of what we do in ministry. I believe ministers deal in prophetic compassion and not counseling in its strictest sense. I agree with Richard Krebs, Ph.D., that *pastors should not be counselors*. The ministry as a profession carries certain "intrinsic failure-producing variables" when ministers try to be long-term counselors. Krebs has identified these variables as transference, role confusion, misplaced priorities, and the promise of cheap growth.[21]

One of the problems in carrying the burden of the "authority" of ministry is that many people project their emotions and fantasies, many from childhood, onto their counselors. Much of this transference can be resolved when the therapist is a detached and objective individual. A minister can never be such a person.

Krebs reinforces what I have discussed in earlier chapters, saying that a "pastor has a variety of roles to perform with . . ." congregants, from teacher to committee participant, to preacher, to confidant. ". . . The client-centered focus that [is] necessary for successful psychotherapy" is almost impossible to maintain. Role confusion is heightened for the minister who trys to play therapist. Krebs goes on to relate that some pastors have left the ministry or have been asked by their congregations to leave particular parishes because their interest in counseling has crowded out the performance of more prosaic church duties.[22]

Finally, it is difficult for the minister as counselor to effect personality changes. Krebs warns:

> Counseling that results in major personality change takes time— years in most cases—and neither the pastor nor their parishioner is really equipped to take the necessary time. . . . The relationship between pastor and parishioner should not have to bear the prolonged psychic rawness. . . .[23]

How, Then, Shall We Counsel?

What should ministers do? People turn to the minister in times of crisis and to turn these people away would be irresponsible. A minister should "evaluate, provide support, and refer"[24] like the *generalist* he or she is! Wayne Oates has written an article entitled "Some Common Sense About the Minister as Counselor." He notes,

Today the quality of both preaching and pastoral counseling rises
or declines in terms of the capacity of the pastor to be a generalist
in pastoral counseling and to synthesize the pulpit and pastoral
ministries. He is not a specialist although our generation has
produced a remarkably capable group of specialists in pastoral
counseling.[25]

Oates describes the minister as "Overseer of a Congregation"
and "Builder of Lasting Relationships." As such, the minister is the
generalist who with prophetic compassion and even anguish does
not have the choice of (1) accepting or discharging individuals in
the way a specialist does,[26] or (2) of specializing in the areas of
personal integration and self-acceptance to the exclusion of working
for the ethical well-being of the kingdom of God. In the building of
relationships, over time, the minister earns his or her power of
prophetic persuasion. Consequently, the minister has a greater
power *and* a greater responsibility with given parishioners than total
strangers working in the speciality of pastoral counseling.

This is a burden. And I know no way around it. This prophetic
compassion over time is a greater burden than the burdens of those
who embrace clinical pastoral education. As I noted previously,
"clinical pastoral education was born in pathology." Dr. Anton Bois-
en, chaplain at Worcester State Hospital and founder of Clinical
Pastoral Education, in 1925 "was joined by his first group of semi-
narians" whom he challenged "to learn from *the living human
document of persons in crisis."* The big difference for the local minister lies in the fact that the human document is different in the
local church.[27]

We focus on individuals in their normal, ordinary, routine pil-
grimages of life, for whom we are probably the only source for
raising their prophetic imagination. The church provides a sociological and theological entity for the person. Rather than studying
documents, then, ministers encounter persons and relationships.
The felt needs of the congregation shape one's ministry while at the
same time the minister must alter ministry to deal with the human
relations needs that may go unexpressed (even unfelt) but are nevertheless real. We can never reduce the agenda to comfort versus
challenge. The real issue is what kind of comfort and what kind of
challenge?

The key, for me, in this issue, is the model of ministry articulated
by Jesus in John 15. Jesus said to his disciples, "No longer do I call

you servants, for the servant does not know what his master is doing; but I have called you friends, for all that I have heard from my Father I have made known to you" (John 15:15).

This model of friendship should be a powerful metaphor in the minister's relationship with the congregation. It follows the foot-washing incident in John's thirteenth chapter. Following the foot-washing, Jesus said, "If I then, your Lord and Teacher, have washed your feet, you also ought to wash one another's feet" (John 13:14).

The images are there of teacher, Lord, and friend. One who teaches is a prophet; one who is Lord is priest and comforter; one who is friend expresses the final and higher image. It is powerful imagery to see Jesus moving away from the exclusive concepts of lordship and teacher and into the more risky concept of friend. Jesus speaks of a relationship that transcends both servanthood and proclamation. Friendship is a liberating theme, central to the gospel and essential for the minister caught on the perch between comfort and confrontation. In addressing this theme in John's Gospel, Jürgen Moltmann writes:

> The relationship of men and women to God is no longer the dependent, obedient relation of servants to their masters. . . . In the fellowship of Jesus the disciples became friends of God. In the fellowship of Jesus they no longer experience God as Lord, nor only as Father; rather they experience him in his innermost nature as Friend. For this reason, open friendship becomes the bond in their fellowship with one another, and it is their vocation in a society still dominated by masters and servants, fathers and children, teachers and pupils, superiors and subordinates.[28]

How then shall we counsel and preach? The minister is called to be the friend of the people, one who proclaims a message of anguish in the midst of a community of grace. The minister's task is that of becoming "friend of the people."

6

Ministers and Friendship Patterns

"This least attractive feature of the ministry is the fact that I have relationships with many people on a professional basis but with few people on a friendship basis." (A fifty-two-year-old male minister)

Because meaningful relationships dissolve loneliness, it is helpful to consider the pattern of clergy friendships outside the minister's family. Several studies indicate clergypersons often experience little clear separation between work, family, recreation, and personal privacy. Consequently there is strong evidence that a large number of parish ministers have difficulty establishing and maintaining close personal friendships, especially ones that are characterized by mutual trust and self-disclosure.[1]

Clergy Friendship Needs

Larry Graham, in an unpublished Ph.D. dissertation entitled "Ministers and Friendship," researched why ministers have difficulty in developing meaningful voluntary relationships. For our purposes, I would like to use his definition of friendship as a "voluntary interpersonal relationship between two or more persons, taking place in the context of shared activities and shared interests, in which mutual giving and receiving takes place over time."[2]

While Graham researched male ministers only, my own research among both male and female ministers supports the existence of Graham's two salient reasons for the difficulty in forming relationships: *political balance* and *emotional freedom*. I also discovered three other areas in which every minister experiences problems: *societal expectations, financial status,* and *time scheduling.*

Given my belief that ministers spend far more time with their work group than secular executives and that this work group understands the nature of the minister's work less clearly than secular work groups understand the work of secular executives, the minister's detachment from meaningful relationships seems inevitable. Consider the problem area of political balance as explained in these words of a sixty-nine-year-old minister who experiences ministry as a lonely job: "You have to be careful not to make a show about how you feel toward people you especially like because it may give them more than their share of power or it may make others jealous."

Closely aligned to the perception of the need for political balance are societal images of the minister and his or her family as the "model" family for the parish or congregation. Who wants to be friends with a model family? On one hand, model families restrict the parishioners' freedom of expression in social gatherings. On the other hand, many individuals in the church feel the need for a "perfect" family and do not wish to have that image shattered. "The people in the congregation have a hands-off policy when it comes to socializing with the family. Also there is the attitude that our children should be experts in the faith" (a forty-one-year-old male minister with three children).

A forty-two-year-old male minister reports that other people's expectations have seriously hampered his family's social life, that people believe "that ministers are people with special holiness or special moral pretensions." A young minister (age thirty) reports, "They expect us to be a model family—socially, spiritually, emotionally. They often find our humanness intolerable (failure, anger, frustration)."

A forty-nine-year-old female minister who co-pastors (full-time) a church with her husband illustrates the dilemma in these words, "We soon learned that the open give-and-take which has been one of the exciting aspects of our marriage had to be done in the privacy of the parsonage."

If these issues were not serious enough in their own right, consider the fact that finances and time schedules most probably would render impossible the efforts of ministers to socialize fully with members of their community even if the "model family" obstacle could be overcome. Before turning to my research for sub-stantiation, allow me the privilege of articulating my own experiences.

The financial state of ministers often precludes the ability of ministers to reciprocate *in kind* with their friends. In the two churches I pastored, I was frequently invited to social outings by lawyers, doctors, and business people who belonged to the church. After a few months in each place it became obvious to me that I could never, on my salary, reciprocate in terms of picking up the tabs in restaurants and inviting those individuals to my home for steak cook-outs or belong to the same social and recreational clubs. The necessity of functioning in a profession where one, at least in a worldly sense, receives "more than one gives" may lead to what Wayne Oates calls "a pauperizing effect, leading one to go through life expecting gifts, looking for help with more than usual avidity, and even demanding special concessions and favors."[3]

The reality of this "pauperizing effect" has been impressed upon me in my relationships with ministers through the Merrill Fellowship progam in Harvard Divinity School. The generosity of Charles Merrill of Boston provides free tuition and a healthy stipend for eight ministers each academic year in order to take a thirteen-week sabbatical from their churches and attend the Harvard Divinity School. The competition is keen for the fellowships, and many ministers who vie for a fellowship have not been away from the ministry for any concentrated period of time in ten or more years.

The first year I was in charge of the program, I was amazed at the incredible demands for special consideration these ministers placed on the staff at the school. More than one angry secretary confronted me with remarks like, "These people think we are their slaves" or "I wish you'd explain to these ministers that they are on equal financial footing with everyone else and we cannot bend the rules for their sake."

Certainly this experience does not happen with every Merrill Fellow, and those ministers who come to the school and expect no favors far outnumber those who do expect favors. I have found it necessary, however, to create two special orientation periods each term to handle the "pauperizing effect" of ministry. The first session is held with the new staff who provide support for the Merrill program. I spend an hour with them explaining that many ministers are used to receiving special privileges from devoted adherents due to the fact that they are less financially rewarded than their professional peers. The other orientation session is held with the ministers themselves prior to the orientation session for regular students. In this session I try to explain that while the fellowship may be a justifiably proud moment in their lives, it does not confer special status on them in the eyes of students and faculty, nor does it obligate staff to perform special functions in order to offset their financial picture, which is as solid as that of any other student.

In my survey of fifty ministers of rather stable and sizeable congregations, only 26 clergy, or 52 percent of the total, were somewhat or totally satisfied with the adequacy of their salaries. Those clergy not satisfied with the adequacy of their salaries cut across all age groupings: 42 percent of those under age forty, 33 percent of those ages forty to fifty-five, and, perhaps as expected, 100 percent of those over fifty-five years of age who are contemplating and in the process of planning for retirement. A full 50 percent of the female ministers who responded to my survey indicated that they feel their salaries are inadequate.

When asked if they believe that other people's expectations have hampered or enriched their family life in ways not experienced by persons engaged in other professions, 20 percent of the respondents specifically mentioned an inability to socialize with friends due to inadequate salary.

Another factor that seriously interferes with ministerial friendship patterns is the fact that ministers work weekends and evenings and usually take their day off during the beginning or middle of the week when most people are working. How well I can remember the difficulties I had trying to find persons in the cities where I pastored who could play golf on Mondays or Tuesdays. And well do I remember long Saturday night drives when I would leave friends at the lake or after a college sporting event in another city so that I could be back home for the Sunday service.

A thirty-six-year-old male minister responds for many of us, "No weekends does not allow a regular time off with other families."

Perhaps this helps explain why, when asked to list their three closest friends, the ministers in my research listed other ministers as composing 51 percent of their nonfamily friends. Other ministers are about the only ones who have the same socialization possibilities!

Consider also the need for emotional freedom. In my work with continuing education in Harvard Divinity School I have interviewed scores of ministers who told me they had been trained to remain somewhat personally detached from parishioners in order to have the emotional freedom needed to minister to those same people in times of crisis or tragedy.

These attitudes are reinforced by the old professional ethical adage that when a minister leaves a parish, she or he is to sever totally the professional relationships with the now "former" parishioners. This attitude continues to be held. Let me quote from the recently published Creative Leadership Series edited by Lyle Schaller. Robert B. Kemper in *Beginning a New Pastorate* writes:

> Before you leave your present pastorate you need to do some things for your successor. You need to make a clean break. Do not come back to your former parish without your successor's invitation to do so. You release and relinquish the convenantal bonds when you resign. Stick to that relinquishment. . . . Bundle the family together, and with tears in your eyes, move on.[4]

That is a wise statement, and I have followed its advice in leaving two parishes. Having been grateful to my predecessors for also adhering to the "ethics of our profession," I am not about to suggest we go against it totally. However, I will admit that the relinquishment of covenantal relationships with work groups plus the need for political balance in volunteer institutions and emotional freedom for effectiveness in crisis situations, create a genuine loneliness in our profession. Often, I wonder if such relinquishment is really necessary.

One of the amazing pieces of data uncovered in Larry Graham's analysis of friendship patterns among vocationally and personally satisfied clergy involves just this issue. Those clergy who were generally effective in achieving their goals in ministry, in whom Graham did not find the loneliness and frustration one usually expects to find in any such study, identified *68 percent of their closest friends as being former parishioners*. My own study of fifty ministers who would be considered successful in the profession identified 56 percent of their closest friends as former parishioners.

Toward Reassessment

I've done some rethinking about some of these issues. Perhaps my conclusions will be "old news" to many of you, but at least allow me to be confessional and play it out. What other profession requires its practitioners to sever covenantal relationships with over half of their closest friends?

Consider the fact that sociological studies of friendship patterns indicate that it takes an average of three years to move from acquaintanceship to friendship. Graham's study shows that the average time it takes for a friendship among healthy and fulfilled ministers to move to a meaningful level is 9.7 years. Couple these findings with the prevalent ministerial career message that when you've been in a parish ten years, that's really too long and detrimental to the "progress" of a church and see where you come out.

The conflicting expectations are evident: ministers are expected to create meaningful relationships with people, in fact, to be "people-oriented"; at the same time they are to refrain from any closeness that impedes political balance and emotional freedom. They are expected to present their families as "model" families to the community, to work on the weekends, to socialize with limited finances, and to exercise care not to reside in the same community too long. Small wonder that research into the friendship patterns of clergy shows that many ministers tend to confide in their spouses about their vocational and personal difficulties instead of in colleagues, close friends, and supervisors even though the spouses provide only limited sources of help in these areas. Confiding only in spouses, of course, places tremendous pressures on the marriages.

Research also indicates that ministers often feel isolated from the support of other ministers. In studies conducted on stress in the ministry, male clergy report that they seek little support in general from their colleagues. Sarah Bentley-Doely writing in *Theological Education* (1972) relates that women clergy say the worst treatment they receive is not from parishioners but from other clergy.[5]

My own research indicates that women clergy are no longer finding as little support as was apparently the case when Bentley-Doely published her findings. None of the eight female ministers indicated that she is somewhat or totally unsatisfied with her relationships with other ministers. However, 47 percent of the male clergy indicated lack of satisfaction in *their* relationships with other ministers.

The amazing thing about prolonged loneliness, which could even lead to depression, is that *at its basic level it is really repressed anger*. Such moments come to us all. We all need recognition and assurances that we are appreciated and valuable. Ministers' positive emotions are often numbed or overridden by the *anger* they feel at not being loved and at an entire system in which career patterns seem to dictate against meaningful relationships.

Two rather amazing results of my research into the friendship patterns of ministers were: (1) the respondents indicated that twenty-two of the one hundred and twelve nonfamily closest friends lived over two hundred miles away; and (2) four of the fifty respondents listed as one of their three closest friends someone who was deceased! Such information was not solicited. I imagine that a large percentage of the closest friends of ministers reside at considerable geographical distance from the ministers.

The presence of dead people on the list was a total surprise to me. Yet, upon reflection, it is plausible. Ministers are most intimately involved with individuals in times of extreme sickness and prior to death. Such involvement adds another burden to ministers. Those with whom they often share most openly and deeply are those with whom friendship patterns are indeed very short and traumatic.

The presence of dead persons on the list might also be explained by the fact that these people were friends from childhood or seminary days. Perhaps no relationships of comparable closeness had been formed in more recent years. This underscores the problem of friendship in the ministry.

So I commend, in addition to family, present and former parishioners as resources against loneliness. I recognize, as I mentioned earlier, that such advice suggests radical reexamination of our clergy career patterns and perhaps even conventional professional ethics. Regardless of the professional costs, we humans must have a social context of ongoing human dependency and honest ventilation of feelings. We must have friends with whom we can express ourselves without fear of reprisal.

One of the first things psychiatrists do with chronically lonely and depressed people is try to get them in comfortable group or individual settings where they can ventilate their true feelings. Ministers need such opportunities as well. Our professional legacy is rich with examples. Jeremiah cursed God publicly on more than one occasion and let his secretary, Baruch, know exactly how he felt about God's failure to respond to developments. Elijah frequently shouted out at God in the presence of his "work group." Jesus of Nazareth on more than one occasion spoke to his disciples (his work group), defining his enemies as "fools!"

Admittedly, such meaningful relationships with present parishioners are fraught with risks. And the prospect of maintaining covenantal relationships with former parishioners seems to be ethical chaos. But clergy can suffer from loss of close involvements with people more than persons in any other profession. Paul H. Olm's recent study titled "Retirement in the United Church of Christ,"[6] discusses the major hurdle presented by removing oneself from the people relationships of the parish. Consequently, of the *active* U.C.C. clergy surveyed, over 50 percent plan to retire within twenty-five miles of their last parish. This data says to me that many ministers at least try to obtain in the latter years of their ministry, when it's ethically acceptable, the close involvement with former parishioners that they would truly like to have enjoyed in the earlier years.

Some congregations, of course, make it easy for pastors to build friendships. But often a new minister is undermined by the friendship patterns of his or her predecessor. Established cliques may expect the new minister to fill the same role as the former pastor or they may reject the new person on the basis of their special friendship with the former pastor.

Building friendships in the ministry is certainly no easy task. I remain convinced, however, that it is not impossible but, rather, is necessary. Just as we begin to function more effectively *personally* when we are intimately engaged with others, so do we begin to function better pastorally when we experience shared intimacy. One cannot be another's pastor unless he or she is willing to become involved with persons at close range and allow persons to know him or her as well.

7

The Burden and the Joy: Economic Sacrifice

Many reports and articles have been written about the clergy surplus and the resulting tight job market for ministers. I am not certain that the so-called "general surplus in clergy" is as much a problem as the surplus of narrow images, expectations, and understandings. We must somehow solve the problem of how people in mid-life can find fulfillment in jobs that are not at the "top" or even close to the "top." It is a lonely experience to serve and run a church in a competent manner, have the years roll by, and, in spite of the security and respect of the work group, become bored and apathetic because one perceives one's function as unimportant and feels that not much is required in terms of expenditure of energy and talent.[1] The supply-demand picture presently mitigates against opportunities for new work; lack of opportunity for new work has a direct impact on the quality of work performance.

This is true in every aspect of work life, not just in the ministry. Professors Stanley M. Davis of Boston University School of Management and Roger L. Gould of U.C.L.A. interviewed more than fifty executives in major American corporations. In one of the published interviews an executive considered himself as having been placed in a job that was lower than the one he had previously held. In his opinion, "It looked impressive on paper," but "you could get a kid to do it." The executive continued, "If you ask me about stress, I will tell you that it is more stressful not to be occupied than to be too occupied."[2]

Without performance, satisfaction declines in any profession; when satisfaction declines, activity is seen as lacking purpose, and that brings one to loneliness. There is perhaps nothing lonelier than feeling that one has become a passive actor in one's own professional future. Contributing to loneliness is the fact that most people tend to compare themselves with those whose rewards or performance are ahead of theirs rather than with those beneath them. When they climb the vocational ladder, they look up, not down.

Clergy Surplus or Economic Identity Crisis?

There seems to be increasing pressure to define purposeful activity in terms of moving to a bigger church. In reality there are many more churches than there are clergy. But many of these are not economically and professionally viable for many clergy. There is no clergy surplus in the smaller churches. But when the career pattern of "bigger is better" takes hold, there is a tremendous over-supply problem. Robert Kemper has identified the problem. "There are more clergy desiring appointment to middle and large churches than there are churches for them, and as long as this pattern holds true there will be a clergy surplus."[3]

I experienced this in a most vivid way. In South Carolina where I pastored, a neighboring church was without a minister. The church was in a rural area, twenty-one miles from a town of thirty thousand people. Eleven of my former classmates in Vanderbilt, Harvard, and Yale looked at the church. Most did not want to live in a rural setting and ruled it out before the search committee progressed very far with them. Two of them felt the two hundred member church was a "dead-end" and too small and insignificant. One minister's wife did not wish to "be stuck there" with farmers' wives twenty-one miles from a city. This couple backed out on the committee after the search committee had even remodeled the parsonage to the wife's specifications. Finally, after fifteen months, the church secured someone with adequate credentials who would tolerate a job in that setting.

Why was the search so difficult? The church served an intelligent constituency, paid a living wage, and was larger than those churches where Harry Emerson Fosdick and Reinhold Niebuhr began their ministries. Yet, in the same way, at Harvard Divinity School, we have many more jobs than students; we have to struggle hard to find students willing to enter the profession at the entry level placements in churches, hospitals, universities, social agencies, and denominational offices.

Conversely, when I resigned the 2,200 member Seventh and James Baptist Church in Waco, Texas, in 1978, the search committee to find my successor had over one hundred unsolicited names submitted to them within six months. This prompted a member of the committee to call me and say, "Boy, I never realized the job market for clergy was so tight. What a surplus of clergy!"

I repeat, there will always be a "clergy surplus" and feelings of stress due to the lack of purposeful activity until the conventional wisdom that "bigger is better" begins to crumble, forcing reexamination of clergy career expectations. I believe that many clergy want to move because they have accepted certain presuppositions about their career patterns which require them to do so. It would be a good resource against loneliness to reexamine those presuppositions. The cost to our profession in terms of trust building and congregational development, both of which take considerable time, is great.

In addition, moving away from friends and pastorates, especially if it is done frequently, can be the cause of much loneliness. The considerable distance between ministers and their friends along with the high percentage of the friends of ministers who are other ministers (as indicated in my research) evidence the fact that ministers, perhaps more than other professionals, live lives characterized by transience.

Hard Choices

The economic pressures on ministers have been well documented. As I have indicated, almost half the ministers I surveyed are dissatisfied with the adequacy of their salaries. Many ministers feel that while they have never taken the vow of poverty, their congregations have taken it for them. Cecil R. Paul has chronicled the following commonly expressed feelings of ministers:

> "The congregation has a double standard: one for the pastor and one for themselves."
>
> "The parsonage stands as the major argument against any cost of living raise—a raise we feel we need in many other ways."

"I drive an old car that many of my congregation wouldn't consider driving, and yet I represent them to the community."

"I wish they would value the sacrifices of time and energy and commitment to care that are central to my ministry. When they lay the financial sacrifice on me, I feel unappreciated."

"It isn't so much the money as it becomes a symbol of how they feel about ministry in general and my ministry in particular."

The pastor's wife communicates similar reactions:

"There is so little we own that is truly ours. At times I long for the freedom of ownership in order to have the freedom to decorate the parsonage and truly express myself."

"My children dress less well than most of the children in the church."

"We have less adequate health care than we ought to have. If we ever face a family health crisis, we will be devastated financially."

"I believe in sacrifice and dedication, too, but I believe God expects us to function as a community and to care for one another."[4]

The image of the poorly paid pastor and the double standard—one for the pastor and one for the laity—has its roots deep in the history of ministry in America. Many a modern-day minister can well identify with the feelings and experiences behind these words of Jonathan Edwards, written in 1734:

"Sir

"By this I would Signify to you that I never have been at so much Difficulty to get in my Salary as I have been this year. Never any Constables were in any measure so Backward."[5]

By 1740, Edward's salary was not sufficient for his growing needs and he could not make his checkbook balance. So he took his case to the town and asked for more money. It was granted. But following an increase the following spring, there grew "a 'great uneasiness in the town' over pastoral expenditures."[6] It was claimed Mr. Edwards was "abusing the generosity of the town by 'lavish' expenditure."[7] "His Boston garb and Sarah's lavish wardrobe and expensive jewelry were a constant source of irritation" with the congregation.[8]

It was tough for Jonathan Edwards to make ends meet financially and avoid the double standard in the 1700s, and it is still tough for men and women in the ministry over two hundred years later.

But unlike Jonathan Edwards, the modern day minister lives in a mass media world. Our television sets, our magazines, our theatres, and much of our advertising present many ideals of financial security. Constantly in our magazines and on our TV screens we see persons who have seemingly attained many of the items we as ministers will never attain. While ministers in other times have, as Edwards illustrates, labored under inadequate salary structures, they and their families at least did not spend hours in front of a television set each week watching apparently exciting lives, tanned bodies, and never-ending supply of money among their contemporaries. In addition, modern media hold before us a new awareness of the prior achievements of those within our own profession. I doubt that an ark on the order of the dimensions of the one described to Noah in the Old Testament could hold the denominational and ministerial periodicals that float over the minister's horizon.

Psychologists have researched a principle called the "adaptation-level phenomenon . . . [which] dates back to the Epicurean and Stoic philosophers of ancient Greece." The principle contends

> that our feelings of success and failure, satisfaction and dissatisfaction, are relative to our prior achievements. If our current achievements are below the neutral point defined by prior experience, then we feel dissatisfied and frustrated; if they are above, then we feel successful and satisfied.
>
> If the achievements continue, . . . we soon adapt to the success. What was formerly positive is now only neutral, and what was formerly neutral becomes negative.

David G. Myers, in his book, *The Inflated Self*, continues, "This is why, despite the rapid increase in real income during the past several decades, the average American is not appreciably happier."[9]

Myers supports his hypothesis with research conducted by the University of Michigan's Survey Research Center which "reports that in 1957 34% of Americans described themselves as 'very happy.' By 1978 our affluence had grown considerably, but, still, 34% said they were 'very happy.'"[10]

Most of us have felt the adaptation-level phenomenon. That's why the new "immobility" in ministry, due to the tight job market at the second and third levels of movement, creates such frustration. Even as ministers contemplate their satisfaction with given accomplishments in present churches and parishes, the satisfaction fades and is replaced by a new level of striving.

Let me make it clear that I am a believer in ministers receiving higher salaries. I am aware that the freedom to become an active actor in your own future is, of course, fundamental in the management of loneliness. And, as everyone knows, this freedom is not simply a psychological freedom; it involves economics as well as emotions. I commend any church that pays its minister a high salary and deplore those that do not live up to their capabilities in this regard. Books abound that offer the minister techniques and information for strategizing with congregations in this regard. I encourage ministers to read them.

But I believe ministers have talked too much about salaries and not enough about utilization of the positive tradeoffs in ministry. While salaries are not exceptionally large for ministers and in many instances have not kept up with the cost of living in the past decade, better salaries are not necessarily the key to satisfaction in the ministry.

What ministers lack in pay is more than compensated for in some of the positive aspects of ministry. In my survey of fifty ministers, forty-one (or 82 percent) clearly comment that their ministry has been fulfilling. Only two indicated that they found the ministry completely unfulfilling. In addition, 76 percent of the respondents were satisfied with the freedom they possess to develop their own life-styles. For example, individuals with financial success in 9-to-5 jobs cannot take an hour or two off on a weekday to see their children in a school play. A minister usually can. Eighty-five percent of the respondents indicated that they are satisfied with the extent to which the ministry fulfills the expectations that they brought to the profession.

Perhaps the most surprising data recovered in my study concerns the extent to which being a minister has actually helped individuals' relationships with their spouses. Twenty-seven of the forty-five married clergy (or 60 percent) believe that becoming a minister has *helped* their marriages. Only seven (or 16 percent) believe that it has hindered their relationship with their spouses. The percentages are consistent among the male and female ministers surveyed and among the ministers who belong to racial minorities!

Among the comments offered to explain how the ministry has helped their relationship with their spouses are these:

> The discretionary time permits a *choice* of time to be together (fifty-year-old male).

A flexible work schedule has helped avoid a lot of problems (forty-four-year-old male).

Training and practice of ministry give me added skills and perspectives in family life (forty-one-year-old male).

It has sensitized me to human needs in her as well as others (forty-eight-year-old male).

Sensitivity and insight into my own marriage are derived from work with others (thirty-seven-year-old male).

Marriage involves the deeper matters of life. Being a minister and aware of them has contributed to making our marriage work (fifty-one-year-old male).

Finally, it appears that more and more congregations are being forced, through economic changes, to recognize the changing trends in terms of both household heads being employed in the work force. Outside of the independence this brings to the minister's spouse (which will be discussed in the next chapter), such arrangements lessen the necessity of focusing too narrowly on the adequacy of the minister's salary for family support. Of the forty-five married ministers surveyed in my research, thirty-two (or 65 percent), indicate that their spouses are employed twenty or more hours per week outside the home. This, of course, represents an incredible change in nature of the perception of the role of the minister's spouse over the past three decades.

Perhaps the minister and his or her family *do* lead a more economically simple life than those individuals in certain other professions. But perhaps ministers should clearly understand the exciting possibilities that are theirs as well. I seriously doubt that one could research fifty established members of another profession and find 82 percent clearly stating that their job is fulfilling, 76 percent clearly satisfied with the freedom they possess to develop their own life-styles, 85 percent satisfied with the extent to which the job fulfills the expectations brought to it, and 60 percent convinced that being in that particular line of work has actually helped their relationships with their spouses! Many individuals in other professions would willingly sacrifice most of their worldly goods to experience such opportunities.

Perhaps ministers need to look with fresh eyes at the value of simple economic living both in terms of the way they relate to the surrounding culture and in terms of their own inner sense of being trapped professionally by the "adaptation level" principle.

Voluntary Simplicity

"Poverty," said Plato, "consists not in the decrease of one's possessions but in the increase of one's greed."[11] While ministers are not greedy, they are human. Many have found the truth in what the senior Rockefeller said when he was asked how much money it takes to satisfy a person, "Just a little more."[12]

In this age when religious television personalities are filling their vaults with megabucks and their crystal cathedrals with people, the concept of the power of volunteer simplicity has taken a back seat, both in society in general and in the ministry in particular. Most of us focus on the joy of stepping up, not stepping down, in terms of status. Yet I am convinced that the apparent clergy surplus, the difficulty of clergy moving to larger parishes, and the economic simplicity forced on the majority of ministers in our culture could well provide the most powerful opportunity to the church to contribute significant theology to our age. In a world where one authority estimates we have approximately 3,000 diet books, 2,000 self-improvement treatises, and over 1,000 sex manuals available to us,[13] the ability of the ministerial profession to live in economic simplicity may hold a key to renewed strength in life.

Earlier in this chapter I mentioned the harsh economic realities in the life of Jonathan Edwards in his Northampton, Massachusetts, church in the early 1700s. Edwards's financial antagonism with the church (or, most probably, the church's antagonism with Edwards over other matters which expressed itself, as in most church situations, with financial attack) led to his dismissal from his church. Most probably, biographers agree, he was a victim of the widespread disagreement between clergy and laity over the matter of authority. What an incredible burden he had to bear! "Under his ministry the church had prospered. He had built the new meeting house. He had seen a generation grow up and take their places in church life. Many of those who now accused him had professed conversion under his preaching. Now, ten to one, they voted for him to go."[14] Jonathan Edwards, who had so steadily looked up the ladder of success, now had to look down it!

It took Jonathan Edwards nearly a year to find another job. Finally, he received a call from a little church in Stockbridge, Massachusetts, in those days a wilderness village. Within three years he died.

Ola Elizabeth Winslow rendered this salient portrait of Edwards's three years in Stockbridge:

> Dismissal from his Northampton pulpit gave Jonathan Edwards his best chance to belong to the ages. In the wilderness of Stockbridge he could preach old sermons to a handful of Indians and a smaller handful of whites, close the door of his four-by-eight-foot study, and make up his mind about the freedom of the will. . . . in this lonely place he would be almost as close to England and Scotland as to Boston. He would be a free citizen of a larger world; not a small-town minister.[15]

I have often thought how much we in the present might have benefited had Jonathan Edwards a decade earlier dealt with his "adaptation level" and actually self-consciously looked "down the ladder" at a more creative, though less visibly prominent, pastoral alternative.

Perhaps ministers in our era will actually benefit from the forced hard choices created by the apparent clergy surplus. I have a colleague who recently "stepped down" from a large Presbyterian church in the Northeast to a church one-fifth its size in a rural area. Although he readily acknowledges the hardships brought about by the reduction in salary—he earns less than half of what he formerly earned—his keen insight commends itself to us:

> For the minister there is a personal dimension to the advantages of the small church. The first thing I noticed was the freedom from stress. This does not always come with the small church. My immediate predecessor experienced more than his share. But I attribute much of it to a lack of experience (He came as a seminary graduate.) which a minister who is stepping down should not share. All of my life I have had asthma. I am allergic to dogs and cats, which are hard to avoid in the parish. Asthma is greatly aggravated by stress. Before I left my last parish my wife, who is inclined to scare easily, was convinced it was going to be fatal. In my present setting it has all but disappeared and is readily managed. I have not yet been able to adapt to this and keep anticipating a stress that has yet to appear. After two-and-a-half years I am beginning to accept the possibility that stress may not be an ingredient in the small church situation.
>
> Another advantage to the ministry is a greater freedom to develop your own potential as you choose rather than having to provide what the demands of the situation require. Previously my continuing education was aimed at learning what I thought I needed to know to do my job. Now it is aimed at becoming what I want to become. The difference is not so much in the content

of the study as it is in the attitude with which I approach it. There is more time for hobbies, for leisure, and for personal development. But the greatest advantage of all is having more time with my family. My wife and I actually spend time together now. Most evenings are our own. When my daughter and her family come to visit, I take time to enjoy my grandson and have no guilt feelings for doing so. Recently I was comparing notes with a urologist who had just made a move similar to my own. I mentioned the salary was half what I had been making but I had a much better home life. He said his experience was the same and added, "Living is better, eating is better, even sex is better." What more could you ask?

I do not claim that the experience of "stepping down" is as promising as might appear from this one example. But if ministers are to break out of the aggressive narcissism of our age they must distinguish between a high standard of living and a high standard of life. They must own simple economic living as a deliberate step in ministry which can promote real happiness and increase their capacity for service.

Richard B. Gregg posits that ". . . it may well be that great simplicity of living is the main condition upon which the learned professions which require leisure will be permitted to exist. If so, the previous voluntary adoption of greater simplicity by the learned professions would count for their security and make the transition easier for them."[16]

Certainly it would be wise to prepare ministers in their seminary experience to visualize the important byproducts of the economic sacrifices necessary in the ministerial task. The Christian heritage as well as the practical realities of the profession demand that they do just that. Voluntary simplicity of living was advocated and practiced by the founders of most of the great religions—Jesus, Buddha, Lao Tse, Moses, Mohammed—as well as the Hebrew prophets.

In speaking of voluntary simplicity, I am not advocating ascetisicm. Nor do I mean the type of Puritan emphasis on frugality that was prevalent in the early history of our nation. Voluntary simplicity is a relative matter. As Gregg articulates: "It means an ordering and guiding of our energy and our desires, a partial restraint in some directions in order to secure greater abundance of life in other directions. It involves a deliberate organization of life for a purpose."[17]

While I do not visualize myself as a zealot for the concept of voluntary simplicity, I believe that any minister who does not examine the strengths available through partial restraint in satisfying one's society-encouraged thirst for economic acquisition is destined for a life of frustration and loneliness.

Part Three

The Minister's Relationship with Family

8

How Are You Fixed
for Family?

James Lynch of the University of Maryland Medical School has conducted some fascinating studies which show that close family and community ties help keep down the number of one's health problems. His research shows that medical practitioners must make people aware that their family life and social life are every bit as important to health as dieting and exercising.[1]

I know of no better way to state it than by citing the irrefutable Old Testament case that paradise without human companionship ceases to be paradise. The biblical account of paradise hardly begins before God is depicted as saying, "It is not good to be alone." Paradise is not enough if in order to obtain it you divest yourself of meaningful relationships. There can be loneliness even in an environmental and vocational paradise.

Many times we have seen ministers build a financially and ecclesiastically strong organization only to realize too late that they have created a monster that robs them of the most precious gifts of life: their family and their friends. Their hates, fears, loneliness, and remorse do not permit them to enjoy the fruits of their labors. Fifty years of prima donna preaching, inspiring choral anthems, majestic sanctuaries, denominational awards and collection plates full of dollars do not stifle or circumvent the pain of a heart longing for meaningful relationships.

As I have noted earlier, our culture, especially the media and literature, has weakened our professional identity among our work group. The more professional identity is weakened, the more crucial become personal and family identities.

In presenting my findings and perspectives on the family lives of ministers, I hope the reader will recall my insistence in earlier chapters that the minister establish nonprofessional and nonfamily relationships. Ministers should never focus on the family as the *only* meaningful area of life. When looking for human worth, confidence, and esteem, "the family" is a misguided reference if it is the sole frame of reference.

The Spouse as Friend

As mentioned in chapter 7, the lives of ministers and their families, in spite of documented studies by psychologists, are not as bleak as one might expect.

I was somewhat anxious to read the doctoral dissertation by Larry Kent Graham entitled "Ministers and Friendship: An Examination of the Friendships Established by a Selected Group of Protestant Parish Clergymen . . ."[2] While the study is regrettably limited to male clergymen, it appealed to me because it analyzed "successful" ministers who are vocationally fulfilled. In fact, 96 percent of the ministers indicated they were finding gratification in their ministry. (Too often we deal with the negative factors in ministry without ever studying as role and process models those who are experiencing fulfillment in the profession.)

As part of the study, these ministers were asked simply to identify, in order of importance, their eight best friends. Amazingly, 56 percent of them regarded their wives as their best friends, even though such a result was not even envisioned or mentioned by the shaper of the questionnaire.

In my own survey of fifty ministers, 45 percent of the married ministers listed their spouses as their best friends even though this choice was not suggested by the questionnaire. All of the married female ministers listed their husbands as one of their three best friends. Two of the eight female respondents, however, are currently separated from their husbands. In addition, 71 percent of the married clergy in my survey responded to the question concerning with whom they talk when they experience intimate problems with "my wife" or "my husband."

Psychologists could perhaps point to these findings, as some have, as indications that ministers are isolated and consequently have few outlets for honest expression outside their marriages. In fact, William B. Presnell writing in *Pastoral Psychology* on "The Minister's Own Marriage," studied fifty-six clergy couples and concluded that most clergy have minimized their family roles and have "difficulty in affirming their human needs, expressing their sexuality and in handling their anger openly."[3]

While I do not take such studies lightly, I believe that psychological studies of troubled clergy have tended to obscure the fact that ministry taken as a whole may produce healthier relationships between spouses than other professions. In fact, my study indicates that the demands of ministry often wear down the rough edges of egocentricity and enable many clergy families to evolve together in unusual internal friendships. There exists as much promise as peril for marriages that operate under the vocational and social structures of "ministry."

The Promise and Peril of the Fish Bowl

Ministers, of course, do live public lives to a greater extent than individuals in other professions. One of the most common criticisms of a ministerial life-style is that the minister lives in a "fishbowl." Volumes have been written about the perils of the "double standard" between clergy and laity, the trauma of being expected to live as a model family, and the tremendous anxiety associated with living before the public as if in a glass bowl.

But I begin with the *promise* of living in the fishbowl because a large number of respondents to my questionnaire articulated *positive* reactions to public expectations in this regard. Frankly, if I had envisioned any response to my question on how ministers perceive their lives as enhanced or hindered by public expectations, it would have been a negative one. I had thought that most ministers would feel public expectations for family life would hamper the minister's family life in ways different from the family life of persons engaged in other professions. But the responses were evenly divided, almost 50-50, between those who felt such distinctions helped their family life and those who felt it hampered family life. Among the positive responses were these:

They (expectations) probably enhanced family life, making me more aware of the importance of family. The expectation that the minister will be a *model* family man probably helped me (forty-six-year-old male).

Probably enhanced . . . Our children became leaders. Our kids are . . . popular at church and get all kinds of stroking (forty-four-year-old male).

Other people's expectations have enhanced my family life. Their faith in me . . . has not only enhanced my family life, but has said to me that what you do is not only important, but helps to set moral and ethical standards (fifty-nine-year-old black male).

I suspect that "church" expectations call you to pay more attention to family issues (forty-one-year-old female).

Privacy is rare/must be circumspect and discreet, although this is probably good for me!! (twenty-eight-year-old female).

My contention that clergy marriages are often better than non-clergy marriages is supported by the findings of David and Vera Mace in their recent publication, *What's Happening to Clergy Marriages?* Over a period of four years (1976 to 1979), the Maces received questionnaires from two hundred married clergypersons. One aspect of that research involved having the pastors and their wives list the advantages of clergy marriage. The items listed by the pastors and wives (anonymously) and the percentage listing each item were:

	Pastors	Wives
1. Shared Christian Commitment and Spiritual Resources	63%	56%
2. Unity of Purpose in Ministering to Others	44%	66%
3. Nurturing Support of Congregation	47%	50%[4]

Such findings are not as difficult to understand as one might imagine. Effective communication is a primary building material in any successful marriage. And effective communication is not an innate talent but a learned skill. Some of the very societal expectations forced on clergy actually contribute to their improved marriages.

The United Methodist Division of Ordained Ministry provided a grant to the Intentional Growth Center at the Lake Junaluska Assembly in 1980 to sponsor a consultation on "The Interface of

Marriage and the Ministry." The findings of that consultation, published in June, 1981, point to this same issue. Charles E. Alexander writes in the findings, "Because of the public nature of the clergy vocation, and because of the varied expectations of congregations toward the minister and partner, clergy spouses in my experience are more quickly and intensely forced to deal with issues of personal identity."[5]

I believe that such struggles, involving pain and requiring sensitive support both from within and outside the marriage, increase marital communication and maturation at an earlier age for individuals in clergy marriages, *especially when those individuals are adequately prepared and forewarned of the issue*. When partners in a marriage are forced to examine the quality of their interpersonal relationships and develop a shared response appropriate to each partner's personality and life-stage, that process of communication is certainly an enhancement to a happy marriage.

Ministry, perhaps more than any other profession, forces its families to establish a mutually shared sense of vocation. David and Vera Mace not only see marriage itself as a vocation but also identify "two clear and distinct, though related, callings . . . to the work of the ministry, [for the minister] and both of them together to the witness they can offer through their marriage."[6]

The vocation of the clergy spouse has changed greatly, of course, in recent years. The traditional vocation of the spouse was to care for and support the one involved in ministry. In this respect the partner (usually the wife) was the one who enabled the clergy partner to fulfill the sacred duties. In this respect the spouse was one who lived on an auxiliary level, a mere appendage of the minister's personhood.[7] As my research will indicate, this situation has dramatically changed in clergy marriages and spouses are no longer being forced to deny their full personhood. Modern clergy wives, as the study by David and Vera Mace and my own study indicate, do not feel that they are under binding obligations about how they will function within the local church. But, such couples do feel that they have a witness to bear together. As persons who are strongly motivated by role and societal expectation to strive for continued growth in their own relationship, most clergy couples find that they cannot offer to others what they do not possess themselves. David and Vera Mace drive to the heart of the issue when they ask:

After all, is it not right and proper for Christians to set high standards for their marriages and family relationships? And wouldn't those clergy couples be happy and grateful if they were in fact living up to these high standards, and measuring up to the expectations of the congregation and of the community?[8]

Clergy and their spouses, of course, are only human and may never reach these goals. But when a couple is committed to a continuing effort to do so, and reaches out to others in the congregation for support, this is not a negative aspect of the vocation at all.

Perhaps the most surprising finding in my research is that thirty-seven of the forty-two ministers who have children are somewhat or totally satisfied with the way they fulfill their role as a parent! When 90 percent of those surveyed respond in this manner, it adds a sense of balance to some of the horror stories about harrassed, hurried clergy who ignore or avoid their children in favor of the church to which they are "married."

On the other hand, the 50 percent who were critical of the fishbowl existence were just as negative as the others had been positive:

> ... The church people feel that they "own" me and I should respond as they wish and when they wish ... Their demands become louder than those of your family ... and one responds to the loudest noise or the greatest threat (forty-eight-year-old male).

> They expect "perfection," which *excludes* being human (forty-year-old male).

> No matter how much it is denied, the minister's spouse is seen as part of a team by many people. We have had problems accepting and living with that. We also got *trapped* by *our own* expectation that others expected us to keep up a front. We live in a "fishbowl" and are aware of it (forty-nine-year-old male).

> Although I am sure that there are similar pressures on other professional life, the pressures on the minister's family tend to be from multiple sides, more encompassing (thirty-nine-year-old male).

Given the obvious mixture in responses, perhaps the most helpful focus would be to identify particular ways in which the "fishbowl" and job-related experiences of ministers and their families differ from similar perils and promises in other professions. Clergy are not alone in finding family hazards in their vocation. Business executives, for example, often find that their families live in a kind of fishbowl, too. The research by Davis and Gould found that spouses of corporate executives tend both to resent their spouses' success in the corporate world and detest the invasion the spouses' vocation make into their private lives. Listen to the words of one such executive:

> I found out last night that the wife of a guy in the company is coming to town, and we're supposed to have them at our house. My wife does not like business entertaining; I'd do a lot more if she did. I'm at the point where she could travel with me if she wanted to, but she doesn't like to. And she's right. Why the hell should she be a prisoner of the company I work for?[9]

To a degree the marital and family-life problems of many ministers do mirror those found in the congregation. The most critical and poignant aspect of the struggle to grow as an adult is the attempt to balance family and work. But the ministry differs significantly in this regard from other professions. The minister operates in a fishbowl which offers less benefits and dollar incentives for more demanding time schedules. In addition, other helping professionals are allowed to solve their family problems as they directly affect individual family members. Clergy family problems, including clergy separation and divorce, seem to involve the entire congregation as well as the denomination.[10]

Another aspect of the ministry that affects family life is the restrictions placed on housing location. Other professionals are not required to live in the community of their employment, much less in a manse or parsonage. Most persons choose a job and then decide where they wish to live so that they can do their work. An executive who accepts a position in New York City frequently chooses to live in the New Jersey or Connecticut suburbs where a family life-style can be maintained that is commensurate with the past history of his or her family. Other persons might work in the suburbs but choose to live in the city close to public transportation, theaters, and other benefits of urban living. But a minister chooses a particular city or section of a city when he or she chooses a job.

If a neighborhood becomes unsatisfactory, another kind of professional can relocate while keeping the same job. Yet if the neighborhood where a minister lives is not suitable, the minister cannot move his or her family to another town or suburb to seek more conducive conditions for family life.

When I accepted a position at Harvard University in Cambridge, Massachusetts, my wife and I chose the community of Walpole,

Massachusetts (some twenty-five miles away from Harvard) as the place where we wished to live. We had friends in the Walpole area and a pediatrician for our child there, and we felt more at home with the professional people there than in the highly transient academic community of Cambridge. Few ministers have the luxury of such choices. For the clergy the place of work must also be the place of residence. For example, the church to which I belong in Walpole has recently called a new minister. If that minister and his wife had wished to live in Cambridge, the church would *not* have called him.

This anomaly about the profession of ministry is a factor in clergy dissatisfaction, especially with the so-called placement system. Placement offices can match the right clergy to the right church, but they are often incapable of matching the right *family* with the right *community*. The right match between person, family, community, and parish is often more than even the best placement system is capable of doing.

In my research among ministers, the second most frequent response for "the least attractive feature of family life" was "the place where we live." In fact, 16 percent of the respondents indicated this. Many voiced the expected complaints about the strains of living in parsonages. These strains focused on the delayed improvements and the sense of dependency that usually accompany parsonage living. Yet others who receive housing allowances are not happy either. Few churches, unlike corporations, will allow the minister to find housing beyond the residential living patterns of the membership. A forty-two-year-old male minister articulates it well:

> What concerns me most is living in an affluent suburb, with few blacks and few poor people. I am concerned that our children may be developing distorted perspectives on the real diversities and problems of living in today's world. I am also concerned that I may be succumbing to a distorted perspective myself, seeing life through the lens of a high achievement, high-pressured, high expectation community.

Other professionals frequently live in a fishbowl, but few outside of ministry live in an *immovable* fishbowl.

Two-Breadwinner Marriages

The family in America is undergoing changes in life-style. These changes affect assumptions about child-rearing and relationships with one's spouse. In 1958, only 9.3 million families were involved in "two-breadwinner" marriages. By 1978 that number had grown to 19.4 million families, and it is estimated that the 1980s will see over 26 million families with both husband and wife as breadwinners. Clergy families, of course, are caught up in the economic stress and societal perceptions that have helped to create this new factor.

My research found that 60 percent of the married respondents are engaged in a two-breadwinner situation in which the spouse is employed more than twenty hours per week outside the home. An additional 9 percent of the married respondents indicate that their spouses work between ten and twenty hours per week in the work force outside the home. Apparently the days are gone when the minister's spouse functioned as an unpaid member of the staff, pouring her (and perhaps occasionally, his) energies into church socials, community volunteer work, and church educational endeavors. This new situation in ministry has its obvious benefits and negative aspects.[11]

If the spouse of the clergyperson is employed outside the home, one of the benefits to the marriage is the fact that the spouse retains a sense of competency and individuality. No longer merely a part of the blended clergy "team," the spouse can develop his or her own vocation and maintain a sense of autonomy. Dr. Bobbie McKay, clinical psychologist, maintains that "a marriage between two individuals who each feel emotionally strong (at least some of the time) is a more effective bonding than a marriage in which one partner is absorbed into the career of the other partner (unless this is an agreed upon situation for both partners)."[12] Clergy responses affirm the truth in this premise.

> Her employment outside the home has meant, on the positive side, a separate identity from the church and the role of minister's wife, a heightened sense of personal worth, and it has enriched the marriage through bringing about new friends made outside the church community (thirty-nine-year-old male whose wife is employed twenty hours per week).
>
> My wife has a real sense of accomplishment in her chosen field and a sense of independence. There is a feeling of happiness when we are together at the end of the day, sharing the experiences of the day (fifty-eight-year-old male whose wife is employed twenty-four hours per week).
>
> The freedom for my spouse from parish expectations is a plus (forty-eight-year-old male whose spouse is employed thirty-five hours per week).

My research also indicates that the spouse who works and feels good about his or her working places fewer expectations on the congregation to provide all or most of his or her emotional satisfactions and affirmations. In addition to the obvious economic advantages (mentioned by 92 percent of the respondents) in the two-breadwinner situation, the situation also can produce heightened family awareness for the two spouses.

> With a working wife, there is more time for the minister (me) . . . to see people and do things that otherwise would be taking time from family. It also lets me relate to my children [directly] rather than through my wife (forty-six-year-old male whose spouse is employed forty hours per week).

> My wife's employment has generally benefited our family life—forcing me to take more of my share of domestic responsibilities and helping our children to become more responsible family members (forty-year-old male whose spouse is employed forty hours per week).

An indication that attitudes are changing among church members is the almost total absence of responses indicating that congregations are critical of the clergy whose spouse insists on working. Only one respondent out of the twenty-seven whose spouses are employed twenty or more hours per week indicated congregational disapproval. To the contrary, 30 percent of the ministers indicated that their spouse's job actually increases solidarity with the congregation.

> Since most of my parishioners are families in which both husband and wife are employed, my wife's employment has assisted us in feeling a part of our community and this has helped my ministry and my appreciation of what other families are experiencing (forty-year-old male).

> That my wife also works outside the home as a teacher does not seem to offend the expectations of the congregation. In fact, since many wives also work, it seems to provide my ministry with a base of solidarity with the congregation (fifty-eight-year-old male).

Lest we too quickly praise working spouses as a panacea for ministerial and personal stress, I note that my research indicates that the lack of time available for family when both spouses work is of great concern. Over 80 percent of the ministers in this category reported negative aspects in terms of time available to be with spouse and children. And *three times* as many ministers in the group of twenty-seven whose spouses are employed indicated that they are "neutral" or "somewhat dissatisfied" with the way they fulfilled their roles as parents than did those in the group of twenty-three ministers whose spouses are not employed. The comments of the former are revealing.

> It (spouse's employment) leaves too little time for our personal marriage relationship (forty-five-year-old male).
>
> I feel that the children sometimes don't get the attention they should because we both work in professions that demand a lot of time (thirty-five-year-old male).
>
> On the negative side, there are sometimes problems with scheduling and child care, a much more complex life-style, and occasional feelings of neglect on the part of our children (thirty-nine-year-old male).

While these time problems are obviously present for a male minister whose spouse is employed, the issue of family life becomes even more difficult for the female minister whose husband is employed fulltime. Many women clergy continue to struggle to be all things to all people: minister, homemaker, friend, wife, and mother. The January 1978 issue of *Theology Today* was devoted to women in the ministry. Among the articles was one by Daphne Parker Hawkes, an Episcopal minister in Trinity Episcopal Church, Princeton, New Jersey. Writing on "Women and the Pastorate," she articulated:

> My own vocational satisfaction is very high, and from conversations with other women I have found this to be true generally. The problems that arise for many of us are in working out schedules that allow us to feel satisfied in our family life as well as in our priesthood. This is a balance that men also have to face, but I think it has new dimensions for the working mother because of the pressures and expectations that are subtly, and sometimes not so subtly, exerted by the culture upon a mother.[13]

The female ministers who responded to my questionnaire remark that theirs is a particularly difficult lot because culture places more family nurturing expectations on the female. In subtle ways, congregants accept the fact that a male minister will have perhaps less influence on his children than will males in other professions. Yet the female minister is not allowed such concessions. When asked to comment on how other people's expectations have hampered or enhanced family life in ways different from persons engaged in other professions, a twenty-eight-year-old married female minister honestly cries, "I am expected to be superwoman!" She then states that the expectation comes not only from others but also from herself. A forty-one-year-old married female minister agrees, ". . . at least I have felt I judge myself more harshly and place greater expectations on my mother-role."

The picture of women in the ministry becomes more complex when one considers that there is no role to adopt *or* react against in terms of male clergy spouses. Most congregations simply "do not quite know what to do with a male clergy 'wife.'"[14] Not only is he probably exempt from traditional church roles of a clergy wife—playing a musical instrument, singing in the choir, participating in the women's association, and so on—but more than likely he is employed fulltime in another situation and is minimally present in the church. Thus the burden of dealing with congregational projections on ministerial family life and nurture, especially in terms of the minister as model family member, tends to fall with double weight on the female minister.

Facing the Giants

Would that I or any other author could offer surefire techniques and cures for the incredible family dilemmas peculiar to the profession of ministry. But I cannot, and such was not the purpose of this book. However, I do believe that the suggestions made in earlier chapters can profoundly improve the quality of the minister's relationships with his or her family.

In addition, I hope that seminary professors who have read these chapters will utilize these findings to introduce reality into the seminary experience. Unrealistic expectations can interfere with job satisfaction and performance. The higher the level of unrealistic expectation carried into a job, the more the potential exists for ultimate failure and disappointment. Any research that can help seminary professors demythologize ministerial life should be utilized, and I hope mine will be. Perhaps we can enable those who enter the ministry to become less vulnerable to the stresses in the profession.

The ministry, as my research indicates, is still caught in conflicting expectations and unrealistic and outmoded concepts of being. In addition, there are many positive aspects of ministry that have been inadequately treated by psychologists who deal only with troubled clergy. On the other hand, certain changes in lay perception, especially with regard to the minister's spouse, are clearly changes for the better.

The ministry is in a period of transition between the prevailing perceptions of the oral culture of several decades ago and the emerging images of today. The ministry today is somewhat like the children of Israel who, after several generations of wondering, stood on the borders of the Promised Land. The spies brought word that the land was inhabited by giants. Some people were frightened and ready to return to Egypt. Others preferred to stay in the wilderness forever, if necessary. After a period of turmoil the entire company was persuaded to take the risks the future held.

The ministry cannot return to the images of yesteryear. New wine cannot be poured into old wineskins. New times demand new perspective and new operational theologies. The ministry cannot stay in the wilderness of uncertainty either.

This book has not pretended to conquer the giant problems that confront us. It has merely sought to raise the issues and clarify some of them. The task of prescribing long-range solutions to the dilemmas, contradictions, and problems that cause loneliness in the ministry must be left to others with greater insight, experience, financial backing, and leisure for research and writing. My only hope is that this effort to identify some of the "giants" and still claim the profession as the promised one, worthy of the risks its future holds, will persuade all of us to move forward in this profession that is much needed in our hurting and needy world.

Appendix

The perspectives and conclusions in the preceding book were supported by and in most instances shaped by my independent research project. With the assistance of my colleagues—Arthur Dyck, professor of ethics, Harvard University, and Sharon Parks, assistant professor in developmental psychology and faith education, Harvard Divinity School—a questionnaire was developed to collect data from ministers concerning the problems and triumphs experienced in the profession. The questionnaire deals with the issues of self-image, professional identity, and family life. The questionnaire is included in this appendix.

The questionnaires were equally divided among the following denominations: Baptist (American and Southern), Unitarian Universalist Association, United Church of Christ, Presbyterian (United Presbyterian Church in the U.S.A. and Presbyterian Church in America), and Lutheran Church in America. In addition, three ministers were surveyed from each of the following: the Episcopal Church, the Christian Church, and the United Methodist Church.

A total of seventy-one questionnaires were mailed with the total number of respondents being fifty, for a response of 70.4 percent. Eight of the fifty respondents were female ministers.

Responses were received from ministers in twenty-two states, the largest number of responses coming from Massachusetts (36 percent), South Carolina (14 percent), Virginia (14 percent), New Hampshire (8 percent), Texas (8 percent), Michigan (6 percent), and Ohio (6 percent). The female responses came from North Carolina, Massachusetts, Virginia, Connecticut, Texas, Ohio, and Toronto, Ontario.

The ages of the respondents are as follows:

under 40 years of age	=	19 ministers
ages 40-55	=	27 ministers
over 55	=	4 ministers

Clergy Questionnaire

1. Identification

   Age _____. Sex _____. Number of years in the ministry _____. Is spouse employed outside the home? _____ Number of hours per week spouse is employed _____. If you are single or divorced, please indicate which _____. Age(s) of children _____.

2. Please check the proper response or offer comment:

   a) I believe that my ministry has been fulfilling _____ not fulfilling _____ other comment _____

   b) I believe that my relationship with my spouse has been fulfilling _____ not fulfilling _____ other comment _____

   c) I believe that being a minister has helped _____ hindered _____ my relationship with my spouse. How?

3. Do you believe that other people's expectations have hampered or enhanced your family life in ways not experienced by persons in other professions? Please comment.
   (If single, please insert "intimate relationships" for "family life.")

4. Please describe your three closest friends, how long you have known them, and in what capacity. (If they are current or former parishioners, please indicate.)

5. What is the most attractive feature of the ministry for you? Why?

6. What is the least attractive feature of the ministry for you? Why?

7. When you experience intimate problems, with whom do you talk?

8. When you experience religious problems, with whom do you talk?

9. If your spouse is employed outside the home, what benefits and problems do you find in the ministry and family life that you attribute to both of you being employed?

10. Do you believe that your congregation understands and appreciates what you do as a minister? Please comment.

11. What is the most attractive feature of your family life? Why?
    (If single, please respond to "your most intimate relationship.")

12. What is the least attractive feature of your family life? Why? (If single, please respond relative to "your most intimate relationship.")

		Unsatisfied		Neutral	Satisfied	
		Totally	Somewhat		Somewhat	Totally
The way I fulfill my role as parent.	NA	1	2	3	4	5
My relationships with other ministers.	NA	1	2	3	4	5
The adequacy of my salary.	NA	1	2	3	4	5
The freedom I have to develop my own life-style.	NA	1	2	3	4	5
The quality of my devotional life.	NA	1	2	3	4	5
The extent to which the ministry fulfills the expectations that I brought to the profession.	NA	1	2	3	4	5

Notes

Chapter One

[1] Fern Schumer, "Job dissatisfaction: Growing every day," *Boston Sunday Globe*, September 28, 1980, p. B12.

[2] See the study conducted by the United Church of Christ. Loyde H. Hartley, "A Study of Clergy Morale" (Lancaster, Pa.: Research Center in Religion and Society, 1980).

[3] James W. Greenwood, III, and James W. Greenwood, Jr., *Managing Executive Stress* (New York: John Wiley & Sons, 1979), p. 27.

[4] Adam Yarmolinsky as quoted in Richard G. Hutcheson, Jr., *Wheel Within the Wheel* (Atlanta: John Knox Press, 1979), p. 39.

[5] I have paraphrased the anonymously authored "What Does a Pastor Do?" The full text may be found in Speed B. Leas, *Time Management* (Nashville: Abingdon Press, 1978), p. 56.

[6] Carnegie Samuel Calian, *Today's Pastor in Tomorrow's World* (New York: Hawthorn/Dutton, 1977), p. 5.

[7] David S. Schuller, Milo L. Brekke, and Merton P. Strommen, *Readiness for Ministry, Volume I—Criteria* (Vandalia, Ohio: The Association of Theological Schools in the United States and Canada, 1975), p. 6.

[8] Margaretta K. Bowers, *Conflicts of the Clergy: A Psychodynamic Study with Case Histories* (New York: Thomas Nelson, Inc., 1963), pp. 3-4.

[9] Suzanne Gordon, *Lonely in America* (New York: Simon & Schuster, 1977).

[10] James Lynch, *The Broken Heart: The Medical Consequences of Loneliness* (New York: Basic Books, Inc., Publishers, 1977).

[11] Edgar M. Grider, *Can I Make It One More Year?* (Atlanta: John Knox Press, 1980), p. 64.

[12] David G. Bowers, *Systems of Organization: Management of the Human Resource* (Ann Arbor: The University of Michigan Press, 1977), p. 10.

[13] "People in Your Neighborhood," words and music by Jeffrey Moss © 1970 Festival Attractions, Inc. ASCAP. Used with permission.

[14] Russell Richey, "The Missing Minister," *Religious Education*, vol. 72, no. 3 (May-June 1977), p. 340.

[15] Peter S. Raible, "Images of Protestant Clergy in American Novels," *Kairos* (Winter, 1979), pp. 11-14.

[16] Eberhard and Phyllis Kronhausen, *Pornography and the Law* (New York: Bell, 1959), p. 217.

[17] Abridged from Ralph McInerny, *Gate of Heaven* (New York: Harper & Row, Publishers, Inc., 1975), pp. 44-47. Copyright © 1975 by Ralph McInerny. Reprinted by permission of Harper & Row, Publishers, Inc. See also the excellent discussion of this work in Ronald Rolheiser, *The Loneliness Factor* (Denville, N.J.: Dimension Books, Inc., 1979), pp. 81-83.

[18] Rollin J. Fairbanks, "Symposium: Clinical Pastoral Education," *Theology Today*, vol. 36, no. 1 (April, 1979), p. 50.

[19] Hartley, *op. cit.*, p. 19.

[20] *Ibid.*, p. 27.

[21] William Glasser, *Reality Therapy: A New Approach to Psychiatry* (New York: Harper & Row, Publishers, Inc., 1965), p. 9.

Chapter Two

[1] Harry Levinson, "When Executives Burn Out," *Harvard Business Review*, vol. 59, no. 3 (May-June, 1981), p. 76. Reprinted by permission of the *Harvard Business Review*. Copyright © 1981 by the President and Fellows of Harvard College; all rights reserved.

[2] Edgar W. Mills and John P. Koval, *Stress in the Ministry* (New York: IDOC-North America, 1971), p. 26.

[3] Christina Maslach, "Burned-Out," *Human Behavior*, vol. 5, no. 9 (September, 1976), p. 18.

[4] Levinson, *op. cit.*, p. 77.

[5] *Ibid.*, p. 76.

[6] *Ibid.*, p. 79.

[7] Mills and Koval, *op. cit.*, p. 3.

[8] *Ibid.*

[9] *Ibid.*, p. 13.

[10] Donald P. Smith, *Clergy in the Cross Fire* (Philadelphia: The Westminster Press, 1973), p. 81.

[11] Stuart G. Leyden, "Coping with Stress," *Church Management—The Clergy Journal* (January, 1981), p. 15.

[12] See Paul Pruyser, *The Minister as Diagnostician* (Philadelphia: The Westminster Press, 1976), p. 25.

[13] R. Alec MacKenzie, *The Time Trap: How to Get More Done in Less Time* (New York: McGraw-Hill Inc., 1972), pp. 10-11.

[14] G. Lloyd Rediger, "Time Urgency," *Church Management—The Clergy Journal* (April, 1980), p. 7.

[15] Henry Sloane Coffin, *Communion Through Preaching* (New York: Charles Scribner's Sons, 1952), p. 94.

[16] *Ibid.*, p. 24.

[17] Cecil R. Paul, *Passages of a Pastor* (Grand Rapids: The Zondervan Corp., 1981), p. 14. Copyright © 1981 by The Zondervan Corporation. Used by permission.

[18] Ann Bartram, "Sexual Intimacy Between the Pastor and the Parishioner" (Highland, Ind.: Creative Audio, 1980).

[19] Mills and Koval, *op. cit.*, p. 25.

Chapter Three

[1] James Luther Adams, *On Being Human Religiously*, ed. Max L. Stackhouse (Boston: Beacon Press, 1976), p. 103.

[2] Donald P. Smith, *Clergy in the Cross Fire* (Philadelphia: The Westminster Press, 1973), p. 142.

[3] George E. Sweazey, "The Place of Ambition in the Ministry," *The Princeton Seminary Bulletin* (February, 1967), p. 36.

[4] *Ibid.*, pp. 37-39.

[5] Justo L. Gonzalez and Catherine G. Gonzalez, *Liberation Preaching: The Pulpit and the Oppressed* (Nashville: Abingdon Press, 1980), p. 23.

[6] Quoted in Thomas E. Brown, "Vocational Crises and Occupational Satisfaction Among Ministers," *The Princeton Seminary Bulletin*, vol. 63, nos. 2 & 3 (December, 1970), p. 55.

[7] Seward Hiltner, "The Minister's Theological Responsibility," *The Princeton Seminary Bulletin*, vol. 2, no. 2, New Series (1979), p. 113.

[8] *Ibid.*

[9] For a short, clear analysis of these terms (as well as operational theology) see C. Roy Woodruff, "Theological Reflection in the Supervisory Process," *The Journal of Pastoral Care*, vol. 34, no. 3 (September, 1980), pp. 197-203.

[10] Adams, *op. cit.*, p. 106.

[11] Paul Tillich, *Systematic Theology*, Volume III (Chicago: University of Chicago Press, 1963), p. 263.

[12] *Ibid.*

[13] Adams, *op. cit.*, pp. 103-104.

[14] Tillich, *op. cit.*, pp. 358-360, 375-376.

[15] James Luther Adams, "Blessed Are the Powerful," *The Christian Century* (June 18, 1969), pp. 838-841.

[16] Edgar M. Grider, *Can I Make It One More Year?* (Atlanta: John Knox Press, 1980), p. 114.

[17] *Ibid.*

[18] Rollo May, *The Meaning of Anxiety*, rev. ed. (New York: The Ronald Press Company, 1950), pp. 216-217.

[19] Robert C. Linthicum, *Christian Revolution for Church Renewal* (Philadelphia: The Westminster Press, 1972), p. 87.

[20] John P. Kildahl, "The Hazards of High Callings," in *The Minister's Own Mental Health*, ed. Wayne E. Oates (Great Neck, N.Y.: Channel Press, Inc., 1961), p. 206.

[21] Linthicum, *op. cit.*, p. 207.

[22] Wayne E. Oates, "The Healthy Minister," in *The Minister's Own Mental Health*, ed. Wayne E. Oates (Great Neck, N.Y.: Channel Press, Inc., 1961), p. 14.

Chapter Four

[1] Speed B. Leas, *Time Management* (Nashville: Abingdon Press, 1978).

[2] John C. Harris, *Stress, Power and Ministry* (Washington, D.C.: The Alban Institute, Inc., 1977), pp. 172-173.

[3] Edgar W. Mills and John P. Koval, *Stress in the Ministry* (New York: IDOC-North America, 1971), pp. 25-26.

[4] Carnegie Samuel Calian, *Today's Pastor in Tomorrow's World* (New York: Hawthorn/Dutton, 1977), p. 85.

[5] Mills and Koval, *op. cit.*, p. 57.

[6] Tilden Edwards, *Spiritual Friend: Reclaiming the Gift of Spiritual Direction* (New York: Paulist Press, 1980), p. 21.

[7] *Ibid.*, p. 29.

[8] Matthew Fox, *On Becoming a Musical Mystical Bear: Spirituality American Style* (New York: Paulist Press, 1976), p. xxiii.

[9] Henry Bergson as quoted by Douglas V. Steere in *On Beginning from Within* (New York: Harper & Row, Publishers, Inc., 1964), p. 10.

[10] Kenneth Russell points to the dangers in spouses being the "soul friend" of ministers in a keen article, "Marriage and the Contemplative Life," *Spiritual Life*, vol. 24, no. 1 (Spring, 1978), p. 126.

[11] Edwards, *op. cit.*

[12] George F. Simons, *Keeping Your Personal Journal* (New York: Paulist Press, 1978), p. 37.

[13] *Ibid.*, p. 62.

[14] Milt Hughes, *Spiritual Journey Notebook* (Nashville: National Student Ministries, 1978).

Chapter Five

[1] Donald P. Smith, *Clergy in the Crossfire* (Philadelphia: The Westminster Press, 1973), p. 26.

[2] Quoted in Robert H. Pfeiffer, "Is the Gospel Obsolete?" *Crozier Quarterly*, vol. 27, no. 4 (October, 1950), p. 294.

[3] Smith, *op. cit.*, p. 35.

[4] Pfeiffer, *op. cit.*, p. 293.

[5] *Ibid.*

[6] Harrison Peyton, "Prophetic Preaching and Pastoral Counseling" (Highland, Ind.: Creative Audio, 1980).

[7] Walter Brueggemann, *The Prophetic Imagination* (Philadelphia: Fortress Press, 1978), p. 13.

[8] *Ibid.* These ideas are explained in more detail throughout Brueggemann's book.

[9] I heard J. Alfred Smith convey this story at the meeting of the Association for Theological Field Educators in Denver, Colorado, January, 1981.

[10] Norman K. Gottwald, *All the Kingdoms of the Earth: Israelite Prophecy and International Relations in the Ancient Near East* (New York: Harper & Row, Publishers, Inc., 1964), p. 85.

[11] *Ibid.*

[12] *Ibid.*, p. 117.

[13] *Ibid.*, pp. 147-209. Discussion of Hosea is found on pp. 119-146.

[14] See especially John S. Holladay, "Assyrian Statecraft and the Prophets of Israel," *Harvard Theological Review*, vol. 63 (1970), pp. 29-51.

[15] See the salient work, H. Wheeler Robinson, *Corporate Personality in Ancient Israel* (Philadelphia: Fortress Press, 1964), p. 21.

[16] H. Wheeler Robinson, *Inspiration and Revelation in the Old Testament* (Oxford: Clarendon Press, 1946), p. 170.

[17] Samuel H. Miller, "A Young Preacher Listens to Fosdick," *Harry Emerson Fosdick's Art of Preaching: An Anthology*, comp. and ed. Lionel Crocker (Springfield, Ill.: Charles C. Thomas, Publisher, 1971), p. 76.

[18] Gottwald, *op. cit.*, p. 207.

[19] See especially Walter Eichrodt, *Theology of the Old Testament* (Philadelphia: The Westminster Press, 1961), Vol. 1, pp. 25-26.

[20] R.B.Y. Scott, *The Relevance of the Prophets* (London: Macmillan Inc., 1944), p. 127.

[21] Richard L. Krebs, "Why Pastors Should Not Be Counselors," *The Journal of Pastoral Care*, vol. 34, no. 4 (December, 1980), pp. 229-230.

[22] *Ibid.*, p. 230.

[23] *Ibid.*, p. 229.

[24] *Ibid.*, p. 231.

[25] Wayne E. Oates, "Some Common Sense About the Minister as Counselor," *MPL Journal*, Inaugural Issue (1978), p. 10.

[26] *Ibid.*, p. 11.

[27] See the excellent article by Robert K. Nace, "Parish Clinical Pastoral Education: Redefining 'The Living Human Document,'" *The Journal of Pastoral Care*, vol. 34, no. 1 (March, 1981), pp. 58-68.

[28] Jürgen Moltmann, *The Passion for Life: A Messianic Lifestyle*, tr. M. Douglas Meeks (Philadelphia: Fortress Press, 1978), p. 57. Also published under the title of *The Open Church: Invitation to a Messianic Lifestyle* (London: SCM Press Ltd., 1978).

Chapter Six

[1] Perhaps the best of these studies is that of Larry Kent Graham, "Ministers and Friendship: An Examination of the Friendships Established by a Selected Group of Protestant Parish Clergymen in the Light of a Working Understanding and Theological Analysis of the Nature of Friendship." Unpublished Ph.D. dissertation, Princeton Theological Seminary, Princeton, New Jersey.

[2] *Ibid.*

[3] Wayne E. Oates, "The Healthy Minister" in *The Minister's Own Mental Health*, ed. Wayne E. Oates (Great Neck, N.Y.: Channel Press, Inc., 1961), p. 21.

[4] Robert G. Kemper, *Beginning a New Pastorate* (Nashville: Abingdon Press, 1978), p. 89.

[5] See reports by Edgar W. Mills and John P. Koval.

[6] Paul H. Olm, "Retirement in the United Church of Christ," June 30, 1978.

Chapter Seven

[1] John C. Harris, *Stress, Power and Ministry* (Washington, D.C.: The Alban Institute, Inc., 1977), p. 121.

[2] Stanley M. Davis and Roger L. Gould, "Three Vice-Presidents in Midlife," *Harvard Business Review*, vol. 59, no. 4 (July-August, 1981), pp. 120, 121. Reprinted by permission of the *Harvard Business Review*. Copyright © 1981 by the President and Fellows of Harvard College; all rights reserved.

[3] Robert G. Kemper, *Beginning a New Pastorate* (Nashville: Abingdon Press, 1978), p. 25.

[4] Cecil R. Paul, *Passages of a Pastor* (Grand Rapids: The Zondervan Corp., 1981), p. 53. Copyright © 1981 by The Zondervan Corporation. Used by permission.

[5] Jonathan Edwards, written across sermon notes dated December, 1734 (Yale Collection) as quoted in Ola Elizabeth Winslow, *Jonathan Edwards* (New York: Macmillan Inc., 1940), p. 215. Copyright 1940 by Macmillan Publishing Co., Inc., renewed 1968 by Ola Elizabeth Winslow.

[6] *Ibid.*, p. 216.

[7] *Ibid.*

[8] Leonard T. Grant, "A Preface to Jonathan Edwards' Financial Difficulties," *Journal of Presbyterian History*, 45 (1967), pp. 27-32.

[9] David G. Myers, *The Inflated Self* (New York: The Seabury Press, 1980), p. 9.

[10] *Ibid.*

[11] *Ibid.*, p. 11.

[12] See Daniel D. Walker, *The Human Problems of the Minister* (New York: Harper & Row, Publishers, Inc., 1960), p. 35.

[13] Myers, *op. cit.*, p. 123.

[14] Winslow, *op. cit.*, p. 241.

[15] *Ibid.*

[16] Richard B. Gregg, "The Value of Volunteer Simplicity," *The Pendle Hill Essays*, no. 3 (Wallingford, Pa.: Pendle Hill, 1936), p. 19.

[17] *Ibid.*, p. 4.

Chapter Eight

[1] James Lynch, *The Broken Heart: The Medical Consequences of Loneliness* (New York: Basic Books Inc., Publishers, 1977).

[2] Larry Kent Graham, "Ministers and Friendship: An Examination of the Friendships Established by a Selected Group of Protestant Parish Clergymen in the Light of a Working Understanding and Theological Analysis of the Nature of Friendship," unpublished Ph.D. dissertation, Princeton Theological Seminary, Princeton, New Jersey.

[3] William B. Presnell, "The Minister's Own Marriage," *Pastoral Psychology*, vol. 25 (Summer, 1977), pp. 272-281.

[4] David and Vera Mace, *What's Happening to Clergy Marriages?* (Nashville: Abingdon Press, 1980), p. 36.

[5] Charles E. Alexander, "The Interface of Marriage and Ministry: A Survey of Annual Conference and Area Directors of Pastoral Care," *The Interface of Marriage and the Ministry*, ed. Miriam Herin (Lake Junaluska, N.C.: Intentional Growth Center, The Lake Junaluska Assembly, 1981), p. 19.

[6] Mace, *op. cit.*, p.92.

[7] *Ibid.*, pp. 92-93.

[8] *Ibid.*, p. 59.

[9] Stanley M. Davis and Roger L. Gould, "Three Vice-Presidents in Midlife," *Harvard Business Review*, vol. 59, no. 4 (July-August, 1981), p. 125. Reprinted by permission of the *Harvard Business Review*. Copyright © 1981 by the President and Fellows of Harvard College; all rights reserved.

[10] I am grateful to the Reverend Bobbie McKay, Ph.D., for her correspondence with me concerning her experience as a psychologist treating troubled clergy.

[11] Again, Dr. McKay's insight was very helpful in my ability to provide a framework for the responses to my questionnaire.

[12] Correspondence with Dr. McKay, July, 1981.

[13] Daphne Parker Hawkes, "Women and the Pastorate," *Theology Today*, vol. 34, no. 4 (January, 1978), pp. 426-428.

[14] Correspondence with Dr. McKay, July, 1981.